A GUIDE TO COURSEWORK IN PSYCHOLOGY

Have you ever had difficulty choosing a research project? Have you ever wondered how your work will be marked?

This book will help students to understand the coursework specifications and marking criteria for a number of key exam boards, including; AQA (Specification A and B), OCR, EDEXCEL, and SQA. It provides specific and highly relevant advice on how to maximise achievement in coursework. Guidance is offered on how best to choose a research project, through to practical advice on how to carry out research and write up reports. Topics to be avoided are also considered and advice is provided on how to navigate the difficulties and avoid common pitfalls.

Key issues covered include:

- An overview of the main methods of investigation in psychology
- Data analysis, including how to present data in Word and Excel and how best to comment on findings
- How to draw conclusions from data and create inferential statistics

Incorporating a series of examples, including an investigation from start to finish, and a laboratory experiment, this book provides clear, practical advice. It will be an invaluable tool for GCSE, AS, and A2 students, helping them to maintain their motivation through coursework assignments and to achieve their potential.

Eamon Fulcher is Senior Lecturer in Psychology at University College Worcester and Visiting Research Professor at the University of Murcia, Spain.

A Guide to Coursework in Psychology

Eamon Fulcher

Psychology Press
Taylor & Francis Group

HOVE AND NEW YORK

First published 2005
by Psychology Press, a part of *T&F Informa Plc*
27 Church Road, Hove, East Sussex, BN3 2FA

Simultaneously published in the USA and Canada
by Psychology Press
270 Madison Avenue, New York, NY 10016

Psychology Press is a part of the Taylor & Francis Group

Copyright © 2005 Psychology Press

Typeset in Palatino by RefineCatch Ltd., Bungay, Suffolk
Printed and bound in Great Britain by TJ International Ltd, Padstow, Cornwall
Cover design by Anú Design

British Library Cataloguing in Publication Data
A catalogue record for this book is available from the British Library

Library of Congress Cataloging in Publication Data
Fulcher, Eamon.
      A guide to coursework in psychology / Eamon Fulcher.– 1st ed.
          p. cm.
      Includes bibliographical references and index.
      ISBN 1-84169-558-0 (hardover) – ISBN 1-84169-559-9 (pbk.)
   1. Psychology–Research.   2. Psychology–Authorship.   3. Report writing.   I. Title
BF76.5.F85 2005
150'.71'1–dc22   2005009819
ISBN 1-84169-558-0 (hbk)
ISBN 1-84169-559-9 (pbk)

Contents

Introduction to coursework in psychology 1

The specifications

The specifications – coursework requirements and the marking criteria – for a number of GCSE, AS, and A2 courses are summarised in Appendix 1. Read the text relating to your course to find out what you have to do and how your work will be marked. It provides you with the coursework details for the following courses/specifications:

- AQA GCSE Psychology
- AQA GCE AS/A2 Psychology (Specification A)
- AQA GCE AS/A2 Psychology (Specification B)
- OCR GCSE Psychology
- OCR GCE AS/A2 Psychology
- EDEXCEL GCE AS/A2 Psychology
- SQA Higher Psychology

Having identified the requirements for your course you can begin reading Chapters 2, 3, and 4 as well as Chapter 9 (*20 ideas for an investigation*), as these will help you choose a topic for your investigation. As you develop your investigation, read the first example report in Chapter 8 since this gives a blow-by-blow account of all the details of a project from choice of topic, to preparation, to the finished product. Chapters 5 and 6 are designed to help you analyse your data and report your results. When you are ready to begin writing up your report, consult Chapter 7, which helps you lay out your work and shows you what to put in each section of the report. It also gives advice on how to write academically and common pitfalls to avoid.

It is no mean feat to carry out an investigation in psychology, but if you adhere to the advice in this book the task will be made much easier for you (and you may even enjoy it!). However, before you delve into the details of the specification for your course, here are a few important points you should know.

Maximising your effort

When teachers, tutors, or examination boards design a course they will also design ways of assessing students, such as through exams and coursework. Nowadays, exam boards and universities have to make every assessment method *transparent*. This means that they have to state what the aims of the course are, what kinds of skills students are likely to acquire, what the marking criteria will be for each item of assessment, and much more. For you, the student, this is a very good thing. First, it should instil confidence in you that the course and the assessment procedures have been well thought out and hence are appropriate for the subject you are studying. Second, it lets you know what the examiner will be looking for when they mark your work. The exam boards publish the marking criteria they will use for all candidates' work. They indicate precisely how many marks will be given for each feature of the coursework. Knowing this will help you to *maximise your effort*.

The way you should maximise your effort in doing your coursework is by directing your effort towards the things that matter *to your examiner*. There is no point in writing ten long paragraphs when only two marks are up for grabs or in writing only two paragraphs when twenty marks are available. By studying and knowing the marking criteria, you will find out where the goal posts are. Hence, you will know where you should be aiming your shots.

So, by reading Appendix 1, you can identify what the requirements are for your course. Knowing what will be expected of you is your first step in trying to obtain the best marks for all of the effort you will be putting into your course. Having read the section relevant to your course you can then refer to the most appropriate chapters and sections in the book. Since not all courses have exactly the same marking criteria (though they are quite similar), you should use the course guide when deciding how the parts of the book will be most helpful to you.

Most items of coursework at GSE and GCSE levels involve an investigation. For this you are required to design a research investigation, to collect data, to analyse the data, to interpret the results, and to evaluate the study. You submit a practical report of your investigation. There are standard ways of doing research and report writing in psychology, and the aim of this book is to give you a solid grounding in them. For this type of assessment, every chapter is relevant. However, some items of assessment do not involve the production of a practical report. In these cases, the nature of the assessment is discussed differently and you are referred to specific chapters for further assistance.

Motivating yourself

This is a good place to offer you some advice about how to motivate yourself (or keep your motivation going). There's no lengthy diatribe about how important it is that you should do you best and there is no attempt to make you feel guilty – just six simple rules:

1. *Don't be a minimalist*. Don't put in just a token effort. Marks worth having require effort worth giving.
2. *Don't be superficial*. Beware of putting all your effort into your presentation. A report has to have *substance*, and no amount of glitter and unnecessary decoration can disguise its absence.
3. *Don't be a perfectionist*. Perfectionism leads to a never-ending cycle of despair. Accept your faults and failings, and everyone else's for that matter, because we all have them. Do your best and not the best that's ever been done.
4. *Be selfish*. The person who has the most to gain from all that effort is YOU! No one is going to fly half way across the world, get into a taxi, knock on your door, and ask you to play for Real Madrid (well, unless you're David Beckham. OK, so I forgot about Michael Owen and Jonathon Woodgate, but that's still only three people out of how many millions?). If you want to get on then you have to get on with it yourself.
5. *Impress yourself*. You should try not to do things to impress others because then you are at *their* mercy – you are like the little pigeon sitting in B.F. Skinner's reinforcement chamber waiting for them to issue their small reward for all your hard work. You should be the master of your own internal reward system. Try to impress yourself and then reward yourself in ways that only you know best.
6. *Don't let time pass you by*. Work out a timetable for each stage of the investigation. Give yourself deadlines and try to stick to them, but don't beat yourself up if you have missed a deadline, just put in a few extra hours of work.

A note on plagiarism

Before we begin discussing the details of a practical investigation, I want to address the issue of plagiarism. The report you submit is expected to be *your own*. Although some courses allow you to collect your data in groups, the report should be written in your own words. If it is not, then you have committed plagiarism, and if your plagiarism is detected you will fail automatically. There are two kinds of plagiarism. The first is a minor transgression where you have copied a paragraph or two from a book or some other source and have not acknowledged the source. As far as the reader is aware, the text is your own since you have not stated otherwise. What you should do in this case is to consider the paragraph as a quotation, insert quotation marks around the paragraph, and mention the author, year of publication, and the page numbers. Here's an example of plagiarism (the plagiarised text is underlined):

> Working memory was first outlined by Baddeley and Hitch (1974). It is a model of short-term or immediate memory, rather than a model of long-term memory. <u>Understanding how we temporarily store and process information is fundamental to understanding almost all other aspects of cognition</u>. The model was designed to account for a number of research findings.

The correct way to present the text is like this:

> Working memory was first outlined by Baddeley and Hitch (1974). It is a model of short-term or immediate memory, rather than a model of long-term memory. According to Andrade (2001), "Understanding how we temporarily store and process information is fundamental to understanding almost all other aspects of cognition" (p. 766). The model was designed to account for a number of research findings.

Very often, such plagiarism is difficult to detect. However when the grammar and the sophistication of the writing suddenly and quite obviously improve, the reader becomes highly suspicious. However, this form of plagiarism is not considered as serious as the second form. This is when a substantial part of the report, or even its entirety, is not the work of the student. This can include: copying whole sections of your report from another source, making up your data, downloading a complete report from the internet and claiming it as your own, and so on.

To give an example, I was once marking a report on an experiment in attention. I will not tell you how I became suspicious, but reading the introduction I suspected that this was not the student's work. I logged onto a database of psychological research reports and typed a phrase from the report into the search engine. Two items by the same authors were listed in the search results. One of these items was a report in a psychological journal I knew was held in my college library. I obtained a photocopy of the journal article and compared it with the student's report. I was a little shocked when I did this because it was not a simple case of copying several paragraphs or chunks from the report – the report had been copied *in its entirety*. Needless to say, the student failed the course. Some students may think it rather mean of me that I publicised the plagiarism to the exam board without first talking to the student or showing some charity. However, it would have been extremely unfair to other students, who had put a great amount of effort into their coursework, not to report this case – I would have done a disservice to those hard-working students. Moreover, since the report was so well written, had I not detected it the student would have got top marks, which would not reflect the student's true ability.

Detecting plagiarism is much easier than many students seem to realise. Every time I have suspected that a piece of work is not genuine, my suspicions have been confirmed. Remember that markers will have read many thousands of student essays and reports. They can tell the genuine article. Furthermore, examiners have access to large databases of reports that you or your school or college may not have access to. Some students may be tempted to pay for essays or reports that they can download from the internet. These students should be aware that examiners too may have purchased membership to such sites.

To sum up, plagiarism is not worth the risk. It is far easier to detect than you may think and the punishment is severe.

The contents of this book

- Your first task is to read the specification (in Appendix 1) that relates to your course and to familiarise yourself with what is required.
- Chapter 2 discusses how to approach choosing a topic for your

investigation. There is more than one way to do this and some you will find more appealing than others. Without a clear approach you can waste hours of your precious study time flitting from one idea to another. This chapter shows you how to focus your efforts and come up with a good design.

- Chapter 3 introduces the scientific method and Chapter 4 outlines the different research designs available to you, such as:
  - The laboratory experiment
  - The natural or field experiment
  - Quasi-experimental designs
  - The correlational design
  - Questionnaires
  - Surveys
  - Observational designs
  - Content analysis

  Some guidance is given, with examples, on how to carry out each of the above designs, how to gather data, and the key advantages and disadvantages of each design.

- Chapter 5 covers the thorny issue of data analysis. Detailed guidance is provided that shows you:
  - How to calculate descriptive statistics;
  - How to create tables in Microsoft Word;
  - How to create graphs for your report in Excel;
  - How to draw preliminary conclusions from descriptive data.

- Chapter 6 covers different types of data you can collect, different types of experimental designs, the logic of using inferential statistics to test hypotheses, and the issue of statistical significance. Each of the most commonly used tests is described (with worked examples). These are:
  - The sign test
  - The Wilcoxon matched-pairs signed ranks test
  - The Mann-Whitney U test
  - The t-tests
  - Spearman's rho
  - The chi-square test

- Chapter 7 discusses how to write up your research in the correct format. It covers everything from how to choose the title for your report, to ways of adhering to the word limit (and what to do if your first draft is over the limit).

- Chapter 8 provides two full reports. For the first report the study is described in detail from the first ideas the student had, to how she overcame a number of problems in the design and organisation of the materials used in the study. The way she approached the writing of her report and how she reduced its word length are also described.

- Chapter 9 lists 20 ideas for a research project. For each I provide some background information, an outline of the main features of the design, and some guidance on which statistics to use.

As you read through this book or work through your research investigation, it is highly likely that you will hit a brick wall. This is a perfectly normal experience when one is acquiring new skills. In this case, please don't hesitate to email me, I'll happily respond. You can be sure that if one student meets a particular type of problem then hundreds of others are having the same problem. It will be useful for further editions of this book to know more about what problems students face when working towards their research investigation. You can email me at eamon@eamonfulcher.com. Also, check out the student pages on my website (www.eamonfulcher.com) for other goodies, such as a Forum where students can post messages about their psychology coursework.

How to choose a 2
research topic

What is this chapter about?

Now that you have identified the requirements for your coursework, you may need to set about choosing a topic. For some items of coursework, it is your tutor or the exam board who decides what the topic is and how to study it. If you are free to choose your own topic then this chapter is aimed at helping you.

In one respect there are clear advantages in having such freedom but there are also several disadvantages. First, you can choose a topic that interests you, and one that you are curious about. You can then set about discovering something of real interest to you. If you are interested in a topic then you are also curious about it and you will wish to find out more. As a result you will enjoy your coursework and hopefully this will be reflected in your final grade. If you are not interested in the topic and it has been given to you, then you are less likely to be curious about the issues involved, and hence less likely to enjoy the work. The disadvantage of having to choose your own topic is that it is not an easy thing to do.

In this chapter we focus on a number of different ways of going about choosing your topic of investigation. We also include a section on ethical guidelines since these are important to know ahead of choosing your topic. Often topics are chosen as a result of reading around a subject. For this reason we discuss how to approach the psychological literature and how reading around a subject or issue can inspire your choice. Finally, some advice is given on which methods and topics to avoid, so that you will be prevented from falling into a deep hole!

Ways to approach your investigation

The top-down approach

We might call the first approach a top-down approach, since we are starting from the top of the problem (thinking about issues and ideas about human behaviour) and working down to the bottom of the problem (thinking about the actual methods we could use). This method is most used by professional researchers. They already have an interest in a particular area and often read articles on the issue. They may support one theory over another and in their reading they identify a new research design with which to pit the predictions of one theory against another.

10 steps of the top-down approach

1. Make a note of an everyday observation on an issue that you have pondered over (such as the truth of the saying, when referring to romantic relationships, "opposites attract") OR make a note of something that you have read on your course that provokes curiosity in you.
2. Read about how psychologists have tried to explain the observation or theory.
3. Read the evidence that has been used to support the theory.
4. Read about problems with the theory, and how it has been challenged.
5. Think about whether any explanation satisfies your own curiosity.
6. Decide to address one of the theories.
7. Choose a research method that could help you address one of the theories.
8. Think in advance about suitable participants and the task you will get them to do.
9. Work out exactly which behaviours are important and how you are going to measure them.
10. Ask yourself whether you have arrived at a design that will indeed put the theory to the test.

If any doubt or pure unprofitable boredom appears at any stage, then start the process again until you happily reach stage 10 (or alternatively ask your tutor's advice – she or he may steer you in the right direction to save you having to think of something else). The top-down approach is the most logical way to proceed and for that reason it is probably easier to achieve a good design with it than with the next method, the bottom-up approach.

The bottom-up approach

The second way of generating an idea is to use a bottom-up approach, where you think about the method before you even think about the topic you want to study. Some students seem to prefer this way. They are determined to use a particular method and with certain types of materials. For example, I recall one student wanting to use the Stroop test when she had no clear idea about the context in which she would use it. There is nothing wrong with this approach; on the contrary, it can lead to some very interesting and original designs, but it can be fraught with difficulty. However, on this occasion it led to an interesting design. You may think the Stroop test would mean that the student would be doing her study on some aspect of attention in cognitive psychology. However, it is quite conceivable that the test could be used in some way in a study designed to test a theory in developmental psychology, or social psychology, or individual differences, and so on. The student in question used the Stroop task as a novel measure of stress. She created two lists of words, stress-related words (crime, money, conflict, etc.) and non-stress-related words (carpet, open, earl, and so on). Each word was written on a separate card and printed in one of the three primary colours. The participant's task was to say the colour in which the word was printed. It was reasoned that the more stressed a participant felt generally, the longer it would take them to work though the cards with the stress-related words than the non-stress-related words. This is because it would be impossible for them to ignore the words on the cards simply because of their stress-relatedness. This would slow them in naming the colours. On the other hand, the non-stress-related words would not interfere with colour naming. An addition to the study was to use two types of stress-related words, one set corresponding to life events and another set corresponding to daily hassles. So, the student then had a design that enabled her to question theories of stress (e.g., those of Holmes & Rahe, 1967, and DeLongis et al., 1982). Let's list the steps involved.

The 8 steps of the bottom-up approach

1. Identify a particular method that you feel would interest you.
2. Read about how the method has been used and the sort of data that can be gathered from the method.
3. Think about the behaviours that are being measured and in which areas of psychology they are studied or discussed.
4. Identify a number of theories that attempt to explain this or related behaviour.

5. Identify supporting evidence for the theory.
6. Identify evidence that challenges the theory.
7. Think about how the method you have chosen could help you test the theory.
8. Modify or reshape the method in a way that is appropriate for the theory you are testing.

Step 7 is undoubtedly the most difficult. How quickly you arrive at an answer to this problem depends mainly on the usability of the method you have chosen. For this reason the bottom-up method may not be the easiest way to approach your study.

The jumping-on-the-bandwagon approach

If you are fortunate enough to know the area or even the topic that you wish to base your study on, then there is an excellent method you could use. This method is also commonly used in psychology by professional researchers. From time to time a new research article is published that presents an entirely new method of investigation. Often, the results reveal something new about behaviour. For example, although short-term memory had been extensively studied from the late 1950s onwards, in 1975 Baddeley and colleagues added something to a standard recall task that was to be repeated often by other psychologists later. A recall task in short-term memory is to present a short list of words to participants who then have to repeat the list exactly as they heard it. What Baddeley, Thomson, and Buchanan (1975) did was to systematically vary the length of each word in the list – some lists consisted of words of one syllable (e.g., sum) and other lists consisted of words of four syllables (e.g., aluminium). They found that participants could recall more short words than long words, which has become known as the *word length effect*. Following the publication of this study, many other researchers could be said to have "jumped on the bandwagon" – they attempted to replicate the effect with one or two variations. Such replications with modifications are extremely useful since it is important to understand such effects, i.e., when they work and how they work.

The 7 steps of the jumping-on-the-bandwagon approach

1. Read *recent* issue of a psychology journal on a topic that you have some interest in.
2. Ignore articles that appear to be modifications of previous research methods.

3. Identify articles that either (a) claim to have discovered a new effect or (b) are unusual or novel in some way.
4. Read the article(s) carefully and identify the method used.
5. Identify the theoretical issues on which the work is based, or the new theory the article may state.
6. Think about the conclusions the author(s) make about the effects or results they have obtained and ask yourself whether, if you changed some aspect of the design, the results would be different.
7. If you think you have identified a modification that could quite dramatically alter the results, then you appear to have found your research design.

Step 3 is the hardest because even if you have found a new effect or novel method it may not interest you. In any case, there is nothing to be lost by spending a day looking through current issues of psychology journals, as you may find out a lot about the topics you are studying for your course. It may be useful advice to make notes while you do this. I have often read something in a new issue that I thought moderately interesting at the time but not worthy of making notes about – only later when the issue reappears in my mind do I wish that I had made at least a note of the journal or the authors!

I have to confess that this is an approach I would recommend if you are willing, because there is something impressive about student work that is based on a contemporary issue. It implies that the student has read to a great depth on the subject and the work reads as very original. Because the effect is so new (i.e., recent) the tutor may be unaware of it and it is almost as though the student has "taken ownership" of it. This is precisely what happens in academic psychology – very often the first paper to have discovered an effect is forgotten, being overshadowed by later research on it.

The straight (or near-straight) replication

Perhaps the most common student practical, either one set by the tutor or one devised by the student herself/himself, is the straight replication. Examples would be to attempt to replicate primacy and recency effects in immediate serial recall or the effects of questioning on eyewitness testimony (e.g., Loftus, 1975).

There are many positives to doing a straight replication. First, the student learns a great deal about research design. Second, by doing the study as a practical, rather than merely being told about it in class or by reading a textbook's version of the study, the student experiences the issue at first hand and hence (a) learns more about it and (b) his or her ability to recall details of the study in an exam is enhanced.

The disadvantages of choosing to do a straight replication are that (a) there is virtually no originality in the work (unless the findings of your study are unusual or your interpretation of the results is particularly insightful and original) and (b) it is not so easy to write a satisfying discussion as it would be if the design was more original – there may be precious little to say on the issue that hasn't already been said in hundreds of psychology textbooks. In this case you are advised to modify some aspects of the design, such as the materials used or the procedure, so that you have provided some original input.

The 5 steps of the straight replication

1. Choose an area or topic that you are interested in.
2. Identify a study that you could *feasibly* replicate.
3. Obtain a copy of the original journal article or a very detailed description from a secondary source.
4. The actual method used in the original study may be rather more complex than is implied by a textbook's description of it, so carefully abstract a part of the design that you are comfortable with.
5. If possible try to modify some aspect of the design, however slight the modification, to add something new to the study (however, make sure that your slight modification is still appropriate for testing the theory that the original study was designed to test).

The straight replication approach is advised for you if you have tried one of the other approaches but have drawn a complete blank, or you are not comfortable or confident with research methods in psychology. One disadvantage, at least for the person marking it, is that it is wide open to abuse. It is very easy to plagiarise a straight replication, that is, copy the text verbatim from the original version or from textbook descriptions (see section on plagiarism in Chapter 1). Another disadvantage is that a straight replication is less challenging than a more original design and this important for the assessor who will be marking your work. You should therefore try to modify certain features of the design or the materials. Replications are everywhere in psychology journals, but in each case there is a slight modification to the basic design. The aim is to test the range of circumstances and the types of materials to which the theory or method is applicable so we can further understand the underlying theory.

The what-planet-are-you-on? approach

This approach is not recommended at all. I have included it for your reference, so that you know what to avoid.

In this approach, you simply ignore everything that you have ever read about in psychology and make up a study yourself – one that has no bearing on anything! Examples might be writing a report about how you trained your dog not to bite the postman's hand, or a diary study of how you failed to lose any weight over a 3-week period. The point is that although one might be able to identify at least some psychological content, there is no *theoretical basis* for the work and there is no *recognised* methodology.

The 4 steps of the what-planet-are-you-on? approach

1. Think about something in your life that someone else might find interesting or useful.
2. Ignore anything to do with academic psychology (and especially research methods in psychology).
3. Do something and write about the something in some kind of systematic way (either as a diary or list of what you did).
4. Sit back and wait for your coursework to fail.

Step 1 is especially difficult for the student, Step 3 is particularly painful for the marker, and Step 4 is particularly painful for everyone concerned.

Other approaches

There are other approaches I have not discussed, such as the guaranteed-to-confirm-your-hypothesis approach, which is a study that tests such an obvious hypothesis that it is virtually guaranteed to be supported by the data you collect (e.g., "A sample of people over 65 will recall fewer trance-music-related words than a sample of 21-year-olds"). The point is that research is about *extending* our knowledge of the world. Furthermore, in science we try to *refute* hypotheses rather than trying to prove ones that are intuitively obvious.

I think it was Posner who once said, commenting on the hard questions in memory research, that we too often look under the lamppost to find our keys in the dark because that's where it's easier to see – but it is in the dark places that we should probably be focusing our efforts. If you have a hypothesis that seems guaranteed to be supported then try to modify your design. Put theories to stringent testing.

Then there is the alphabet-soup approach, in which a non-standard research design is chosen and one that seems to have very little to do with the introduction, or where the results section brings in all manner of statistical techniques that are near impossible to decipher. This approach is written by students who appear to be in a total state of confusion. My advice is to keep your investigation simple, try not to be overly ambitious, and read through the sections of this book slowly and carefully.

Finally, there is the ethical-nightmare approach, of which there are many variants. In this design, the student adopts the antiquated stance that he or she as a psychological investigator can assume the right to conduct any inquiry they wish for the sake of the advancement of knowledge. Typically, in such an experiment, a participant is distressed, embarrassed, humiliated, held against their wishes, and so on. Worse still is when little Johnny, who found the task so difficult he burst into tears long before the investigator lost his temper, brings his parents into college the next day wanting answers and demanding action. The message here is to completely understand ethical issues before letting yourself loose on an unsuspecting public. Don't assume that ethical issues are intuitively obvious – there are many potential pitfalls and you need to be aware of them before you begin your study rather than afterwards. A subtle and more covert variant of the ethical-nightmare approach is when a student decides that he or she doesn't like the look of the data they have gathered. The only solution, they deem, is to tamper with a few numbers and perhaps the two bars on the graph might separate a little more. Do *not* be tempted to do this. The purpose of research is to understand people, the mind, and behaviour, and when we invent data we learn nothing.

Methods and topics to avoid

There are a number of topics I would advise you to steer clear of for various reasons. Note also that for the OCR course there are more stringent guidelines on what is and what isn't allowed.

Sexual orientation or sexual behaviour
Clearly you cannot use a question such as "Are you straight or gay/lesbian?" in your study. You have no right to ask such a question either to a complete stranger or to someone in your school or class. Similarly, you have no right to ask other questions about someone's sexuality or their sexual behaviour. To steer your study away from potential ethical problems avoid sexual orientation and sexual behaviour.

Pictures or other materials of an offensive nature

You should not show your participants photographs of a sexual nature, those involving some form of physical mutilation, or those that some people may find disgusting. Similarly you should be careful about using text that your participant may find offensive. If you have chosen pictures or text that you feel may be of concern, however mild, (and your study has been approved) then the best safeguard is to inform participants in advance of the nature of the photographs and that they should not take part if they believe they may find the material offensive. An example is using photographs of spiders in a study of spider phobia. Looking at a close-up of a spider may seem nothing to you but may be disturbing for others (including me!).

Animals

The testing of animals is covered by the BPS (British Psychological Society) code of conduct. The code is particularly detailed in terms of the keeping and treatment of animals. You may keep animals yourself and think that they are a suitable topic for your investigation. However, as opportune as this appears, I would still advise you to avoid a study on animals.

Over-reliance on other people

Diary studies and repeated testing (with intervals of days or weeks between testing) can be quite useful methods for certain topics, such as everyday action slips or long-term memory. The main problem with them is that many of your participants may fail to keep accurate records or may fail to show up. Your coursework is therefore at the mercy of other people's diligence. An important rule in choosing your method and the task for your participants is *do not allow your coursework to be at the mercy of other people*. If they let you down then you may miss important deadlines.

Physiological tests

Some students think that under the umbrella of a coursework investigation they are allowed to do anything they wish. However, there is a strict code of conduct (see later section on ethical guidelines) on the way you should treat human participants. In terms of physiological recordings, it should be obvious that extracting blood or any other substance from your participants is inappropriate. Three big problems with taking physiological recordings are (i) the equipment is very expensive and access to it may be difficult, (ii) most equipment requires some training and in many cases this can be very time consuming, (iii) most physiological recordings are data intensive and may require you to examine very large data files (in many cases it can take longer to abstract the data from such files than it can to test your participants). Therefore, you need to think carefully before embarking on a study involving physiological recordings.

Feigning an accident or crime

The method whereby students go out into the street or other public place, and faint or create a mock crime or a mock accident, can be a lot of fun. However, it can be fraught with difficulties and should be avoided at all costs. Suppose that a passer-by thought the accident was real. They may react with alarm and they may take unusually dangerous risks (to you or to themselves) in taking action. You have no right to put someone in this position.

Conformity

It is unlikely that you would be given any sort of approval for a study on conformity, such as a replication of one of Solomon Asch's studies. Such studies are almost guaranteed to make your participants feel stupid, uncomfortable, anxious, embarrassed, or guilty.

Social facilitation

Some exam boards will not allow your study to be based on any form of social facilitation. This is where the behaviour of someone is motivated by the presence of an audience. The reason is that it would be very difficult to avoid making at least some of your participants feel stupid, uncomfortable, anxious, embarrassed, or guilty.

Interviewing children

Children differ in how they react to being asked what are, to them, weird questions. Some children can be quite sensitive. The way you react to their comments could easily make them feel stupid or embarrassed. What right do you have to make them feel that way? If you do insist on using children as your participants then you must think very carefully about it. Try to make the exercise fun or interesting for them (but do not reward them with sweets). Alternatively, avoid any potential effect on them by observing them from a distance, with permission of course. In any eventuality, you must adhere closely to the ethical guidelines (see later) and you must seek approval from your tutor, the school, and the parents of the children. The simplest advice is to avoid using anyone under 16 as the subject of your study.

Substance abuse

I would strongly advise against basing your investigation on substance abuse. Most drugs that would form your topic of investigation are likely to be illegal. If you studied the users of such drugs you could find yourself in some difficult situations.

Doing a literature review

I have inserted a section on doing your literature review in this chapter because, very often, students read around a subject before choosing the precise nature of their investigation. Furthermore, the act of doing a literature review can inspire you greatly and can be very informative in terms of the design to choose for your study.

Research usually begins with a question. Why do people do what they do under certain circumstances? It is for you to identify the behaviour and the circumstances in question that will form the basis for your coursework. You do this by reading around an issue and by finding out how other psychologists have investigated it. This may sound rather daunting and you might be tempted to base your study on something you read in an introductory text in psychology (or even a newspaper or magazine!). However, be aware that if you don't do much reading, then:

1. You won't be able to "locate your study in a broader context", meaning that you won't know what other relevant research has gone on before. However, your teacher or tutor will, and she's the one who hands out the marks.
2. The report will be very difficult to write because you won't have much to say. In this case you may well be tempted to (a) repeat yourself throughout to make up the word count and/or (b) write about beautifully trivial things that are at best vaguely related to your study.

My advice would be to think about an issue you have read about on your psychology course that interests you. Make sure that it *does* interest you, since you are about to spend many hours thinking and reading about it. Read your course textbook carefully to get a good overview of the issue, and identify further reading (either from the book or from your tutor). Another good source for obtaining a decent overview of a topic is the BPS's journal *The Psychologist*. These reviews of research areas are usually written to get you the reader interested in an area and to lead you to further reading. When you feel you are

become more violent and aggressive towards the prisoners, and many students acting as prisoners became very distressed at the situation. The study showed that the adoption of a role (e.g., guard) can have a major effect on the way a person behaves, even to the point that their previous self "becomes unrecognisable". If you want to look at this study in more detail and with pictures, see http://www.zimbardo.com/zimbardo.html

In both of these studies (and there are many others) many participants were distressed, some close to mental disturbances, and one has to question what right a researcher has to cause such distress in volunteers who have found themselves involved unwittingly in an extremely disturbing experiment.

There are now strict guidelines in force and it has become ever more apparent that tight controls need to be in place for psychological research and the treatment of its participants.

What this means for your coursework is that you will need to adhere closely to published ethical guidelines. Otherwise, apart from the misery you could induce into other people as well as yourself, you will almost certainly fail your coursework.

You can obtain more details of ethical guidelines from the British Psychological Society's (BPS) website at www.bps.org.uk or from the Association for the Teaching of Psychology's website at www.theatp.org/Ethics-Teachers.html. Another resource for ethical issues is located at www.psychology.org/links/Resources/Ethical_Issues

The BPS code of conduct for conducting research with human participants is printed in the section "Ethical principles for conducting research with human participants" available at: www.bps.org.uk/documents/code.pdf

Rather than paraphrase those guidelines (and hence be in danger of misrepresenting them), I have included some extra comments of my own below that you may like to consider (the numbering refers to the numbered points in the guide itself).

Comments

- 1.2 The emphasis here is on mutual respect between the researcher and the participant. Also note that sometimes we just have to accept that some areas are out of bounds for research owing to the likelihood of breaching ethical codes.
- 1.4 Although it seems unlikely to happen for student project work, participants may wish to take legal action against you or your school/college if their rights have been infringed.
- 2.1 You should consider your investigation from the participant's

point of view. Is there any threat, or danger of a threat, to their psychological well-being or physical health? You must also include a consideration of their dignity; they must not feel humiliated, insulted, or embarrassed by taking part in your study. A very important point is that while you may feel that there are no ethical problems with your study, you may not be the best person to decide. You may not know how someone of a different age, gender, or social background might feel towards your study. So, always seek advice from your target population: for example, if you are male and your study is on women's attitudes, seek advice from women about whether the materials are offensive in any way.

- 3.1 While you need to inform all participants of the purpose of your study, there is one problem area. In many cases, if they knew the hypothesis then this would affect their behaviour and the results may be meaningless. In this instance you are allowed to disguise the hypothesis but only if, on being told the hypothesis afterwards, your participants are neither upset nor insulted in any way. See also section 4 on this issue.

- 5.2 This is an important point. Just because you intend to debrief your participants does not make your study OK.

- 5.3 It may be a good idea to provide a rationale of your study on paper, which you give to participants afterwards. Remember too that if someone scores particularly highly on a questionnaire then they do not need to be alarmed by this. Most questionnaires have little diagnostic validity (although some do of course) and you should never give advice selectively. One safeguard might be to provide all your participants with a leaflet published by a recognised organisation or society that informs them about the issue you are studying. If a participant asks for your advice about their personal health or well-being then you must indicate that you are not qualified to provide such advice, but you should have identified in advance an appropriate source of professional advice for them.

- 6. A rule of thumb is to make it clear to participants that: (1) they do not have to provide any information that they regard as too personal if they so wish, and (2) they have the right to withdraw from this study at any time, *without giving a reason*, and without any penalty whatsoever. You should state these verbally and in print so that your participants are fully aware of this. Don't just go through the process as if you don't really mean it, since this might inhibit participants from withdrawing or withholding personal information. An example of the point about not penalising participants is if you decide to pay your participants a nominal fee, then make it clear that they will still get the fee even if they withdraw (and if their intention was just to pocket the money and not take part, then that is the price you have to pay).

- 7. It may be quite possible for a reader of your report to identify the participants even if you have taken many steps to achieve confidentiality. For example, if your study involved participants with specific characteristics, it may be possible for others to work out who these people are. In addition, if you used students in a class from another school or college it may be possible for your reader to identify individual participants if you have named the school. However, it is safe to say in your report that, for example, the participants were all from a school in the region of Hertfordshire.

An important point is that if your study has been approved by your tutor or even an ethics committee, then you are bound by that design – the approval is for a specific design with specific materials, and any changes to the design or materials will need fresh approval.

You always have to ask yourself: Do I have the right to ask people this or find this out about someone? Even if you wear your heart on your sleeve, this does not mean to say that you should expect other people to reveal very personal things about themselves. You must also ask yourself whether you have the right to get someone to think about certain issues. For example, do you have the right to get someone who is very happily married to question any aspect of his or her marriage or relationship?

The points made above should hopefully reveal to you that questions of ethics in research are not always obvious. Common sense is not always the best guiding principle. Personally, I would recommend that any research you undertake has ethical approval from your teacher or ethics committee at your school or in the institution from which you may be recruiting. Indeed, if you are studying students at a different college or workers from a local factory, always insist that the establishment vets your design on ethical grounds. Never carry out research without seeking advice from your teacher, tutor, or other appropriate member of your school or college.

Information sheet and consent forms

When recruiting your participants you may need to obtain permission from an institution, school, or workplace. You should therefore write to them formally to obtain permission and, ideally, you should obtain a letter from them if they decide to support your project. In addition, you should provide a consent form for your participants to sign (and/or their parents/carers). This proves that you warned your participants ahead of the study and it also serves to raise their awareness that their participation is voluntary and that they have the right to withdraw from the study at any time. Give your participants an *information sheet*, which gives an idea of the investigation you are doing (although it is not normal in psychology to inform your participants what your hypothesis is) and what they are expected to do, before giving them a consent form to sign. If you are required to obtain permission from a school or other organisation, include the information sheet and consent form with your letter.

Example consent form

Consent Form for Participation in Research

My name is _____ and I am 18 years or over and I consent to participate in the research described to me on the information sheet for the research investigation titled [insert the working title of your investigation here] and carried out by [enter your name here] for her course [enter the course name here] at [enter the name of your school or college here].

Details of the procedures and any risks have been explained to me and I agree to allow the information obtained from me, my behaviour, or my performance, to be analysed in the report for the coursework.

I understand that:

- I am free to withdraw at any time and without giving a reason.
- I can refuse to answer a particular question or divulge certain information if I so choose.
- Whether I participate or not, or whether I withdraw during the investigation or not will not affect my own course results in any way.

I have had the opportunity to discuss taking part in this study with a friend or member of my family.

Signed _____ Date _____

Research in psychology 3

What is this chapter about?

In this chapter the rationale of research in psychology is discussed. Differences between quantitative and qualitative methods are outlined and we describe the process of developing a research question and a research hypothesis. The chapter also gives advice on how to obtain willing participants for your study and the different ways of taking measurements from them.

Quantitative versus qualitative methods

The adjective *quantitative* refers to the noun *quantity*. Something that has quantity has an amount that can be *measured*. An object has a quantity of weight (e.g., 3 kilograms) and it has a quantity of size (e.g., 1.5 metres in length). In psychology, we usually try to measure behaviour. In doing, so we assume that behaviour can have a quantity (we say that we are trying to quantify behaviour). If this assumption is correct, i.e., that we can quantify behaviour, then we can convert observations of behaviour into *numbers*. Once we have numbers, we have data, and we can use statistics. In other words, by transforming behaviour into data, psychology can adopt scientific approaches and methods in trying to understand human and animal behaviour. Most research in psychology is done using quantitative methods.

Here's an example. Suppose we want to develop an understanding of anxiety. If we want to use a quantitative method then we need to ask ourselves whether anxiety can be quantified. Think about the occasions you have felt nervous. You may have trembled a little, you may have sweated quite a lot, you may have found that your breathing rate increased, and your heart may have been pounding. Each of these bodily feelings associated with anxiety may be measured. So, sweating can be measured through an electronic device that records changes (even very small changes) in the amount of sweat on the skin.

Sweat conducts electricity. Therefore, if two probes are placed close together on a part of the body (say, the palm of the hand or a finger), then it is possible to measure the electrical current between them. The more sweat, the more current that is able to pass between the two probes. This current, and any changes to it, can be measured electronically.

Now, although we would be able to record physiological changes to the body during an emotionally intense state, such as anxiety, what would we say about our internal experience of anxiety? For example, we feel apprehensive and afraid. What do the words "apprehensive" and "afraid" mean in the context of experiencing anxiety? How can we quantify a feeling of apprehension? We might say that it is what one feels when one is expecting something unpleasant to happen in the immediate or near future. This description of apprehension is *qualitative*. It describes, in words rather than in numbers, something as a *quality*. However, we may be able to measure apprehension through a related behaviour. For example, suppose we wanted to measure apprehension in adults. We could show them two boxes, one green and one red, and tell them that in the green box is something unpleasant, though it isn't dangerous, and in the red box is something pleasant. It would be reasonable to assume that if they are apprehensive about opening the green box then they will take longer to open it than the red box. Thus, the extra time taken (in seconds) to open the green box could be used as a measure of apprehension. We have inferred apprehension, a qualitative state, from a measurement of the time a behaviour takes (a quantity).

This illustrates a key point about quantitative methods in psychology. Many of the measures we take involve an inference: we infer a psychological state that is difficult or impossible to measure from a related behaviour that is easily measured. When designing a psychological investigation that uses a qualitative method, an important question is then how to turn or transform something qualitative into something quantitative and measurable. There are more examples of how psychologists do this in the descriptions of the different methods below.

Now you may feel that the qualitative state of apprehension is something more than just delaying the experience of something unpleasant. The reduction of such a psychological state into numbers might in this sense be less than satisfying to an investigator, or even inadequate. Some psychologists are against the notion that behaviour can be converted into numbers, while others wish to explore textual data (the things that people say about their internal states or the world around them). Such researchers opt for *qualitative* methods. In addition, many qualitative researchers wish to explore how concepts are understood within social discourse (e.g., conversations). By doing this, it is argued, we learn more about how people construct their understanding of the world around them and how they construct their own identities. Some examples of these are:

- *Discourse analysis.* The focus of discourse analysis is the conversation (the spoken or written word) and the main topic of interest is the underlying social structure contained within the conversation. The investigator draws no inferences about intentions and motivations of the individuals having the conversation, but rather attempts to identify categories, ideas, views, roles, and so on, within the text itself. The researcher uses the transcript of the conversation (a systematic way of coding the words) as their source. Examples might be mother–child conversations focusing on anxiety-provoking situations, or a conversation among a group of factory workers about the royal family.
- *Ethnographic research.* In ethnographic research the investigator takes him or herself into a situation, such as a group, and becomes part of it. The investigator puts aside his or her own beliefs and values and observes the group or situation. Documents may be read, conversations listened to, and people may be interviewed. Notes are taken throughout about the investigator's observations and their own reactions to them.
- *Action research.* In action research, the topic of investigation typically surrounds a particular problem, how it arose, and how it might be solved. The effects of any solution found will also be examined. The investigator may use questionnaires, discussion groups, and interviews, as well as examining documents and observing situations.

Most courses require you or expect you to use a quantitative method and for this reason we will focus only on quantitative methods.

Which design should I choose?

Remember that in Chapter 1 I said that your goal is to obtain the maximum marks achievable by you. So, although an investigation with a sophisticated design might look impressive, if it is not carried out very well or not reported on clearly, then it will have a disastrous effect on your marks. Likewise, if you are confident with sophisticated designs and choose a simple design that only vaguely assesses a theory then you are not going to maximise your chances of high marks. I would suggest four rules of thumb:

1. **Be aware of your own abilities, strengths, and weaknesses**. In choosing and designing a method, ensure that it takes full advantage of what you are good at doing, and choose a level of sophistication in your design that you can handle.
2. **Prefer a simple or relatively simple design to a sophisticated design**, if the more straightforward design can provide a convincing test of a theory.
3. Only increase the level of sophistication of a design by an amount that is sufficient to provide a convincing test of a theory. **Never choose a sophisticated design for the sole purpose of trying to impress**, especially if its ability to test a theory is weak or unclear.
4. Usually **one hypothesis is sufficient**. Focus your data collection on measurements required to test the hypothesis. Two or more hypotheses don't really add a great deal to a report, but they can easily overcomplicate matters. Don't be tempted to take a whole range of measurements from your participants if many of those measurements are unhelpful in testing your hypothesis.

Finally, remember that the more complicated your design is, then (a) the more difficult it is for you to write about and evaluate, (b) the more statistics will be involved (with an unlikely gain in marks), and (c) the more difficult it will be for your marker to read and understand.

The aims of the investigation

The main aim of psychology is to determine the causes of behaviour. This assumes that behaviour is determined by either:

* *Internal states*, such as a person's mood, their personal experiences, hormonal changes, what their goals are, their perceptions of the world and other people, and so on.
* *External situations*, such as where a person is (at home, at work, at play, and so on), whom they are with, and details of the situation.

In determining the causes of behaviour, psychologists develop explanations or theories. These theories attempt to account for particular types of behaviour in particular circumstances. A popular theory can be adopted in a number of practical settings, for example in determining the best way to bring up a child or the best way to teach a large class of children. Since theories can have such a large impact, it is important that they are good, i.e., near to the truth. The costs of implementing a popular, though bad, theory can have broad, unpleasant implications. Since anyone can dream up a theory of human behaviour we need an efficient and reliable way of discriminating between good and bad theories.

The purpose of a quantitative investigation is to test the validity of a theory, i.e., whether it is a good one or a bad one. With this in mind, you should always think about your investigation as a test of a particular theory.

Can the findings of an investigation prove a theory?

Theories can be broken down into series of predictions or hypotheses. These predictions are tested in an investigation. If the findings are in agreement with the prediction then is it not tempting to say that the theory has been proved to be correct? The problem with the notion that theories can be proved is that a completely different theory could have made the same prediction. For example, suppose my theory is that the reason why we dream is to come to terms with unpleasant experiences, and hence avoid depression. I could make the prediction that people who do not dream are more likely to be depressed than people who do dream. Of course, my prediction will be supported since people who are depressed find it difficult to sleep in the first place! So although my theory could be supported by research findings, it may still be a bad theory. At best, we can say that the findings are *consistent* with the theory.

Can an investigation disprove a theory?

If the findings of an investigation do not agree with the predictions of a theory, then it is equally tempting to conclude that the theory has been disproved. The problem with the idea that theories can be disproved by one investigation is how do we know whether the investigation was sufficiently designed to provide an adequate test of the theory? Suppose, in testing the theory that dreaming helps us reappraise bad experiences so that we avoid depression, I compared depressed people on medication with people with no symptoms of depression. It may be the case that people who are depressed and taking medication sleep more than my sample of people with no symptoms of depression. In this case my prediction will not be

- People with a high "attachment score" will also have a high "needs trusting love score".
- People with a low "attachment score" will also have a low "needs trusting love score".

We could also make predictions about what should *not happen* with our data:

- People with a high "attachment score" will *not* have a low "needs trusting love score".
- People with a low "attachment score" will *not* have a high "needs trusting love score".

The above predictions can be conveyed in one sentence, which is our *hypothesis*:

- "Attachment scores" will correlate positively with scores on "needs trusting love".

If we carried out such a study and found a positive correlation between these two, then we would have *supported the hypothesis* and in turn we would have provided some support for the theory. If we found no positive correlation then we would have failed to support the hypothesis and we would say that our findings are inconsistent with the theory. Note that the hypothesis has the following features:

1. It is a prediction of the results of the investigation.
2. It is precise, in that it says exactly what the nature of the correlation is (whether it should be positive or negative).
3. It is unambiguous, in that the hypothesis can be interpreted in only one way.

The only difference between this hypothesis and the one from the previous example is that here the prediction involves a *correlation*, whereas the previous hypothesis involved a *test of differences* (which group will score higher than which other group).

If you are required to use inferential statistics (see your specification in Appendix 1) then the test of the hypothesis is your correlation test (such as the Pearson test of correlation). However, if you are not required to use inferential tests then you can plot the scores as a scattergraph.

In all quantitative methods, we have at least one hypothesis that we aim to test. In some cases, such as in an observational study, we may have more than one hypothesis. For example, if we recorded say three different types of behaviour in our observation, we may wish to have three hypotheses. It should be the case that the three hypotheses are based on testing the same theory or two competing theories.

Your participants: Samples and populations

A population, in scientific terms, is a pool of people with certain characteristics (or *parameters*). It does not necessarily refer to the population of a country. One could speak of a population of 9-year-old children, or a population of depressed bank managers. These would refer to either every 9-year-old in the world or every depressed bank manager in the world, respectively. A population can be defined by a few parameters, such as the population of all females, or by many parameters, such as the population of anxious radar operators with an attentional disorder.

It is very easy to forget that an experiment or survey you have devised may be limited in terms of its application or generalisation to the population. This is because we cannot test *all* of the population, but rather we test a *sample*. If we were interested in studying radar operators, it is unlikely that we would be able to test them all. Instead, we select a sample of radar operators for our study and then attempt to generalise our findings to all radar operators. Furthermore, we may attempt to generalise our findings to other populations, such as railway control operators.

Generalisation to other populations may not be possible. A reading task designed for experienced readers may be unsuitable for small children, individuals with a visual impairment, non-English speakers, and so on. So we define our target population as people with certain characteristics (population parameters) for whom the effect we are studying would be appropriate. In an ideal investigation, the sample will be *representative* of the population, that is, individuals in the sample will be typical of the population. So, if 75% of radar operators are men then 75% of our sample should be men. If our sample is unusual, in that it does not really represent the population, then we will have difficulty generalising our findings to the population. We can attempt to obtain a representative sample by knowing what the population parameters are (knowing the male to female ratio, the age range, and so on). We can ensure that we have a sample as similar as possible to the population.

However, this supposes that (i) we know all of the population parameters, (ii) all of the population parameters have relevance for the effect we are studying, and (iii) obtaining a representative sample is feasible. In many cases none of these applies.

An alternative is to obtain a *random sample*. Members of the population are chosen for your study randomly. Often we cannot choose randomly from the entire population, but rather we can identify a group or representative sample and select randomly from that sample. Random selection is useful since it rules out any unwitting systematic bias you may introduce into your selection process (e.g., you may accidentally choose children with interesting last names). In one of my own studies, based on 7-year-old children, I identified 10 schools that were willing to take part in the study. These were fairly representative of the population, in that there was a mix of rural and urban schools, and some schools were located in poor areas, while a handful were private schools. I selected about 5 children from each class of 10 to 15 children whose parents had agreed to their taking part. The way in which the children were chosen was through random selection. In this way I ruled out any bias the teacher (if I had allowed her to make the selections) or I may have had in selecting the children.

One problem with random selection is that I may not have access to the entire population but rather a subset of the population, so my sample is not a truly random sample. In my study on 7-year-olds, the schools chosen were local to my place of work. My sample may therefore have been biased by the fact that they were only from a certain area of the UK. Furthermore, some schools did not wish to take part (for example, due to conflicting timescales) so I could not select from them.

A common alternative is the *opportunity sample*. You simply accept the difficult practical aspects of obtaining a representative sample and just go with those you can get to agree to take part in your study. An example is a psychology researcher at a university who chooses her own students as her sample. These participants may not be representative of the population or randomly chosen, but at least the researcher has a sample and if the results prove to be interesting then one could always see it as a pilot study for further investigation. The point is, be clear in your report about how your participants were selected and show that, however you have chosen your sample, you are aware of its limitations.

Measuring your participants

Given the above discussion, it is important that you describe the selection method in your report and that you describe your sample statistically. If they were college students then you need to state which college they were from and which course they were studying, provided that this would not breach confidentiality (in that the reader could work out who the individuals were that took part). It is standard practice to provide the male/female ratio (e.g., "75% were men"), the age range ("aged between 19 and 21 years") and the average age ("with a mean age of 19.7 years"), and the standard deviation of the sample ("and with a standard deviation of 2.6"). You also need to mention any impairments that are relevant to the study, such as how many wore glasses, how many were colour-blind, how many suffered from dyslexia, and so on, depending on the task they were given. So, in a study on the perception of colour it may be important for the results of your study to know if any participants were colour-blind. The point is to describe the task-relevant aspects of your sample.

How do you obtain participants?

If only there were an easy answer to this question! You could offer money, if you had plenty of it! However, some people respond to other inducements, such as knowing that they are likely to contribute to knowledge or that they are making a small contribution to your career. In my experience, a good group for this is retired people and you may like to consider targeting them in your recruitment process (if age is not an important population parameter!). The most likely sample for your study is your classmates, but remember that since you are familiar with them you need to consider the ethics of your study (especially in terms of asking them to reveal personal information or finding out about their abilities, which could prove embarrassing). Obviously the way you obtain your participants is dependent on the population to which your study is applicable. If you require a specific sample then here are some hints:

Children from local schools.   Be sure to contact the school well in advance of the time you wish to carry out the study. Obtaining permission from the school and consent from parents can be a slow process. A good idea is to contact any previous school you have attended or any school where you are familiar with one of the teachers. You could even write to a school that you have no connection with, in the hope that they may be willing to consider your study. In any case, you should write to the head teacher to make your request formal and you should provide details of your study, such as your main aims, the task the children will be doing, how you will select your sample, and details or examples of any materials you will be presenting to the children. You must allow time for the teachers to discuss your proposal, and remember that they are under no obligation to help you. If your proposal is approved you will then need to write to each parent or guardian to obtain their consent. Remember, this must be an 'opt-in' rather than an 'opt-out' request.

Mother and toddler groups. As with schools, when choosing a mother and toddler group you can base your selection on those groups that you have some familiarity with. However, obtaining permissions will be different. Those who run the group may give permission in an informal way and leave it up to individual parents. In this case you should provide as much detail about your study as possible, bearing in mind that if the first parent declines then it is likely that other parents will follow suit. Conversely, if the first few parents agree then there may be pressure for other parents to take part. You should not exploit this. Instead you should contact parents individually, so that they make their own choices privately.

People at a workplace. This can be a very good source of volunteers, and is most useful when you know someone who works in a place where there are many volunteers to be had. However, there are a few things to consider. First, you should not encourage the volunteers to be tested inside working hours (unless you have clear permission from the employer) but rather in their lunch break, for example. You could easily get them into trouble with their employers. Second, it should not be the case that the employer, acting on your behalf, coerces his or her employees to take part. This would breach the code of voluntary participation. Third, it should not be the case that you uncover personal information about people who, although unknown to you, may be well known to the contact at the workplace. This would breach the code of confidentiality.

People in the street. If you are planning a survey or questionnaire, then people in the street may be an opportune sample. You should always carry some form of identification with you so that people know whom they are talking to and the institution you are from. Remember that you will be perceived as representing your school or college, so you should be clear that this is *your* study not the college's. Finally, by approaching strangers in the street you are increasing the risks to your own safety. It is therefore not advisable to be alone – always have someone with you (ideally, a nightclub doorman look-alike!).

People on the internet.   Online discussion forums are a good source for carrying out a survey or questionnaire. If you have access to one, or know someone who could find out how to access one, then this approach might yield many respondents. Another idea is to create an online questionnaire yourself (if you have the know-how) and to place it on your personal home page, if you have one. In fact, there is a free online service where you can create your own questionnaire or survey and download the results. Visit http://www.my3q.com/misc/register/register.phtml

typically the *one difference* between two groups of participants. In other words, the two groups of participants are required to do exactly the same task, except that there is one and only one difference between the two groups. In the example here, it is whether they are allowed to rehearse or not. In every other aspect, the task is identical: the same words are used, the same number of words are presented and in the same format, and the amount of time spent reading the words should also be the same.

The *dependent variable* is a precise measurement of performance that you take from your participants. For example, it may be the number of items correctly recalled from a list of words shown previously.

The experiment is set up so that the effects of the independent variable can be seen on the dependent variable. More precisely, if an effect is present, then there should be differences in the dependent variable between participants who differ on the independent variable. For example, there may be differences in the number of words recalled between participants given the opportunity to rehearse a list of words and those not given the chance to rehearse the items.

The importance of controls

In order to have confidence that any effect found is the effect of the independent variable on the dependent variable, the two groups must not differ in any other way, other than the independent variable itself. How can we know that they did not differ in some other way? The answer is to use *controls*. These are modifications to the method that ensure, to the best of our knowledge, that the task is as similar as possible in all respects but one for the two groups. To do this we define our groups as an *experimental group* and a *control group*. The experimental group carries out the positive feature of the task, and for the control group this positive feature is absent but the task is otherwise the same (and as similar in procedure as possible).

For example, we may wish to compare the effects of rehearsal on the recall of a list of words. We define a task for two groups of participants that is identical, but then add the positive feature to the experimental group and remove that feature from the control group. We may want to encourage the experimental group to rehearse the list of words and to prevent the control group from rehearsing the list. We need, therefore, to devise a method that prevents the control group from rehearsing the items. One way is to get the control group to do another task after the list has been presented, such as counting backwards from a given number in threes (e.g., 346, 343, 340, 337, 334, and so on). They are given a specific amount of time to do the counting task, say 10 seconds, before they are asked to recall the list of words. Now, for the experimental group we allow them the *same amount of time*, i.e., 10 seconds, to rehearse. It has to be the same amount of time because if this differs between the two groups, then we have introduced an extra difference between them (the time delay between being presented with a list and being asked to recall it may influence the amount of information recalled). Time is therefore a controlled variable.

So, the task given to the two groups is identical, except for one, and only one, aspect. In addition, the situation in which testing takes place has to be identical for both groups: the lighting, the location, the instructions given to them, and so on. If one group were tested, say, just after their lunch break and the other group were tested, say, just after a particularly difficult maths lesson, then the first group might be more relaxed and less tired than the second group. Such differences between the two groups are known as *confounding variables*. We design our experiments using controls to minimise the risk of introducing confounding variables.

Independent groups design

The type of design we have just been discussing is known as an independent groups design, because we have two different or independent groups of participants, the experimental and control groups. The obvious problem with this is that the two groups may differ in important ways. For example, one group might simply have better memories than another group. This is known as a *subject variable* (because it is some ability or characteristic on which the two groups of participants can differ). If the two groups did differ in their ability to remember things, then any effect of the independent variable (the role of rehearsal) on the dependent variable (the number of items recalled) may become obscured or eliminated by the presence of the confounding variable.

Random allocation into groups

It is generally assumed that the way to avoid confounding variables within your sample of participants is in the method of allocating participants to each group. One method is to *randomly allocate* each participant into his or her group. For example, if you require 12 participants in each group, you write "experimental group" on 12 small pieces of paper and "control group" on another 12 small pieces of paper, put them all into a hat, and get the participants to dip their hand in and choose one piece of paper. The idea is that if you randomly allocate participants then you will tend to even them out in ability. You can try this yourself: get 24 people to write down their height and then choose their group (experimental or control) out of the hat in the way just described. Then add up the heights of the experimental group and find the average height. Do the same for the control group. The prediction is that the average heights of the two groups will be very similar. Of course, this works provided you do not have one person in the sample who is particularly taller than the rest, and/or one person who is particularly shorter than the rest. The problem with random allocation is that you are leaving it to chance whether your groups are about the same in ability.

Matched groups design

Another way to avoid subject variables is to deliberately match the participants on ability. For example, you could give all participants a simple memory test and then make sure that the two groups are matched by the measurement of memory you have taken. Each group will be about equal in the numbers of people who have strong and poor memories. The main problems with a *matched design* like this one are that (a) it is time consuming and you need to test *all of the participants* on the ability test before you can test any one of them on the main task of the experiment, and (b) you may have matched them on one ability but there will be other abilities on which you have not attempted to match them that may be important for the type of task used in your study.

Repeated measures design

A third method is to use a repeated measures design. In this design you do not have to concern yourself with individual differences between the groups – you use the same group of participants for both "conditions". So, rather than have two independent groups (an experimental group and a control group), in this design there is an *experimental condition* and a *control condition*. For example, all the participants do the memory task with rehearsal (experimental condition) and then all of the participants do the task with no rehearsal allowed (control condition). Of course, having eliminated one problem, others are introduced. For example, the participant may have learned something about the second condition having just done the first, or the participant may have been affected by the first condition and this may have either a beneficial or a detrimental effect on the second condition. These are known as *carryover effects* or *order effects* and they include the effects of practice and fatigue. For example, a practice effect occurs when the participant has had some practice on the first task and therefore does better on the second task because of this practice. An effect of fatigue occurs when, having done the experimental condition, the participant is too tired and worn out to do the control condition properly. Clearly this will adversely affect the results. Practice and fatigue effects are confounding variables. One way to reduce the effects of practice or fatigue is to divide your participants in half – one half does the experimental condition first then the control condition second, while the other half does the control condition first then the experimental condition second. Of course, you have not eliminated practice effects (because they are still getting benefit from whatever task they do first) but what you have done is to *control* for practice effects, by making sure that the same task is not made easier by practice for *all of the participants*.

A second problem when using a repeated measures design is with the materials used. If the same material is used for the two tasks, then clearly doing the first task will affect performance on the second task. This is another type of order effect. In the example we have been using, the word lists should be different for the two tasks. However, this may be unsatisfactory since one list of words might be easier to learn than another list. The way to reduce such effects is through *systematic rotation* or *counterbalancing*. The idea is that you create all possible combinations, so that you even out or eliminate any particular bias that would make performance in one condition superior to any other instance. See Figure 4.1 for how we could use rotation to eliminate practice effects and any order effects in the list of words used. A further concern would be any differences between the two lists. Ideally the experimenter makes the words as similar as possible (for example, in terms of their length, how often the words are used in everyday language, and so on).

Standardised instructions

It is important to give participants clear instructions as to what to expect, as you do not want them asking you lots of questions during the task. It is common to write out the instructions beforehand and either read them out or let the participants read them for themselves. Another important reason why you might choose to write your instructions down is so that every participant in each group or condition gets the same ones. If different participants are given slightly different

Figure 4.1. Control for order and practice effects. The participants are divided into four groups. Each group does the task in a different order with a different set of words. For example, Group 1 do task A with word list 1 first, then they do task B with word list 2. This way word list 1 is used half of the time with task A and half of the time with task B; word list 1 is also used in the first task half of the time and in the second task half of the time. Task A is studying a list of words with rehearsal, and Task B is studying a list of words with no rehearsal.

Group	First task	Second task
	Task A with:	Task B with:
1	Word list 1	Word list 2
2	Word list 2	Word list 1
	Task B with:	Task A with:
3	Word list 1	Word list 2
4	Word list 2	Word list 1

instructions they will behave in slightly different ways, and this is undesirable.

You should begin with a "thank you", and then go on to tell your participants about the task ahead. Tell them how many trials to expect and the general area of the research. In most studies of experimental psychology you do not tell them your hypothesis, as this can affect their behaviour. Although this can be construed as a slight deception, it may be difficult to avoid. Always end the instructions by telling participants that they have the right to withdraw from the experiment at any time and without giving a reason. For an example, see Experiment 1 in Chapter 8.

Choosing a design

The design that you choose for an experiment will depend on many factors, but whichever you choose you have to take numerous steps to avoid confounding variables. No design is perfect, and one must always accept that this will be the case. Your task will not be to create the perfect design; on the contrary, showing your examiner that you fully understand how to use controls for confounding variables is your main task. So, if you know there is a confound but cannot do anything about it, then mentioning it in the report will still get you marks.

Types of tasks: Inferring something psychological from behaviour

In any experiment, we will wish to infer something psychological from the behaviour of our participants. However, the behaviour must be measurable – we must be able to assign numbers to behaviours. This then allows us to gather and analyse data. We can then decide whether the analysis supports our experimental prediction.

The most common forms of measurement in experimental psychology are the following.

Reaction time or time taken to respond

- If one task takes more time to complete than another task (and the response is similar) then it is fair to assume that the first task involves greater cognitive processing – either deeper thought or just more thought.
- *Example*: if it takes longer to solve anagrams of long words than it does to solve anagrams of short words, then we infer that solving long-worded anagrams involves greater cognitive processing than solving short-worded anagrams.

- *How to record reaction time.* Usually psychologists record reaction time using a computer, which can record reaction time in milliseconds. The computer is also used to present the materials to the participants. However, you can use a stopwatch, but this is only useful if two different tasks in your experiment are likely to take noticeable differences in time to respond. One method is to get participants to do 10 trials of the experimental condition and time them for the whole 10 trials. Then time them for 10 trials on the control condition. For each task you can then find the average time on each trial (by dividing the time taken by 10). You can then compare these means in your results.

Number of errors

- Very often the number of errors the participant makes at some task is used in conjunction with reaction time. However, it can be used by itself. Generally we can infer that if participants make more errors on Task A than on Task B, then the cognitive processes involved in Task A are more complex than those in Task B. Typically, participants may be prone to some form of interference, hence the errors.
- *Example*: The task for the experimental group involves doing maths with someone counting in the background. The task for the control group involves doing the same maths as the experimental group but with someone reading words in the background. If participants in the experimental group make more errors than those in the control group, then we have demonstrated an interference effect of the sound of counting (but less so for the sound of words) on the cognitive processes involved in doing maths.
- *How to record the number of errors.* You should ensure that the two tasks (groups or conditions) are as similar as possible, there being only one difference between the two tasks (the independent variable). Make sure that there is the same time limit for both tasks. Do not allow participants to complete a task through to the end with no time constraint (if someone has sufficient time they can easily avoid errors). An important point here is to avoid ceiling and floor effects. A ceiling effect occurs when hardly anyone makes an error (performance "hits the ceiling"). A floor effect occurs when hardly anyone gets anything correct. Your tasks should be "discriminating", in that you need a good spread of scores, with few participants making zero errors or having zero correct. The key here is to pilot your method: try it out on yourself or friends before testing your participants. If you find that the task is too easy or difficult you can then make changes to it before spending time on testing. If

Rating scales

- Rating scales are used when we wish to obtain information about emotional or attitudinal states, or about perceptual judgements.
- *Example*: The experimental task involves rating the degree to which a photograph of an emotionally ambiguous face displays displeasure. The control task involves rating the degree to which the same photograph displays pleasure. A collection of 30 photographs of human faces is used. If the experimental condition yields higher average ratings than does the control condition, then we can infer something about the detection of positive and negative emotions in faces, namely that it is easier to detect displeasure than pleasure in a face. Suppose we gave the task to one group of people who have just watched a sad movie and another group who have just watched a comical movie. Suppose further that the sad-movie group had higher ratings for the experimental condition than the control condition but there was no difference in ratings between tasks in the two conditions for the comical-movie group. We could then infer that being sad makes one more predisposed to detect negative emotions rather than positive ones.
- *How to use a rating scale*. The best way to present the scale to participants is visually. The scale should have clearly marked points, the number of which is up to you – the more points on the scale the greater spread of scores you should obtain. Each point can be labelled numerically, e.g., from 1 to 10, or textually, e.g., "I dislike it a lot", "I dislike it a bit", "I neither like it nor dislike it", "I like it a bit", "I like it a lot"). If using a numbered scale the extremes need to be labelled (e.g., "Least liked" and "Most liked"). The participant can either write down a number corresponding to the point on the scale or they can mark the scale themselves. See Figure 4.2 for examples.

Advantages and disadvantages of experimental methods

As we have discussed above, the main advantage of the experiment is that it allows us to test a hypothesis in a *controlled* environment (such as a laboratory). The experimenter can control:

- Who the participants are.
- The tasks the participants are required to do.
- The sequence of events in the design.
- A good number of confounding variables.
- The variables in the study.

Method 1. A numerical scale with labelled anchors

The participant enters a number corresponding to the scale:

Picture 1	3
Picture 2	5
Picture 3	2

Method 2. A completely labelled scale

The participant could provide a verbal response, which you record.

Method 3. A numerical scale with labelled anchors, which is also used to record responses.

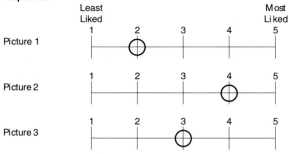

Such control enables the experimenter to isolate *cause and effect relationships*. However, all of this control can have disadvantages:

• The behaviour under study may be rather artificial and unusual for the participant.
• Everyday behaviour may be difficult to study in an experiment.

An alternative method to the laboratory experiment is to conduct an experiment in a person's normal environment. In field or natural experiments, people are studied doing their usual activities in their usual environment; the experimenter takes little (but some) control over the situation.

Variations of the laboratory experiment

The natural or field experiment

In a field experiment, the experimenter observes people in their usual environment but manipulates one or two aspects and notes the effects this has on behaviour. There are two main ways of manipulating the situation:

- The manipulation can be subtle or *covert*, in which a "stooge" or "confederate" of the experimenter acts in a certain way and the behaviour of others is noted. An example is a study of aggression where the stooge sits in a car at the front of a queue at a set of traffic lights. When the lights turn green the stooge does not move and the behaviour of the others in the queue is observed (such as tooting their horns, flashing their lights, waving their fists, shouting through the side window, and so on). Note that this study is not without its own ethical problems!
- The manipulation can be more direct and controlled, in which a new system or procedure is introduced into the environment. An example is a comparison of a new method of training with an existing training method. The investigator then compares the results of a test or exam for the two training methods.

The clear advantage of this approach over the lab experiment is that people are behaving in their usual way and in their usual environment. Hence the behaviour being measured has greater validity (see later section on reliability and validity).

The disadvantages of the field experiment are:

- There are likely to be several ethical concerns. First, it is a usual requirement that participants are willing volunteers in an experiment. However, in a natural experiment they may not even be aware that they are in an experiment. Second, covert manipulation (such as not moving when the lights turn green) may cause people distress or to behave in ways that represent a danger to themselves or other people (such as having a heart-attack or punching someone as a result of the incident).
- There is a danger that the manipulation may interfere with the

normal operation of an organisation or institution. For example, the introduction of a new training method may interfere with normal practice and may have detrimental effects (especially if the training method was less effective; the trainee "guinea pigs" would have lost out).

Quasi-experimental designs

A related technique is to use a quasi-experimental design. The word "quasi" here means semi or partly. The main difference is that in a quasi-experiment it is not possible to randomly allocate participants into groups. For example, if you wish to conduct an experiment on sex differences, you cannot randomly assign participants into groups of men and women! The problem with not randomly assigning participants is that we increase the chances of having unequal groups – groups that may be very different in terms of a range of abilities. In a quasi-experimental design the participants fall into naturally occurring groups (such as men and women, pregnant teenagers and non-pregnant teenagers, retired bank managers and employed bank managers, and people who wear seatbelts and those who don't).

Correlational designs

The main difference between a true experiment and a correlational design is that whereas in the former we can infer causal relationships, in correlational designs we can only detect associations. By association we mean that two variables are related in a systematic way – as one changes so too does the other. Examples of correlations include weight and height (the taller someone is, the weightier they are likely to be); A-level grades and degree classifications (the better you do in your A levels, the better the class of degree you are likely to achieve); intelligence between parents and their children (the more intelligent the parent, the more intelligent the child is likely to be). There are also *illusory correlations*, such as between the probability that your printer will develop a fault and the urgency of the work you are printing out, or the severity of your hunger and the number of tasty snacks in the cupboard (although for me these correlations seem pretty reliable!).

Correlation is measured as a value on the scale -1 to $+1$. The minus sign indicates a negative correlation and the plus sign indicates a positive correlation. A correlation close to 0 implies no correlation. A positive correlation describes a direct relationship between two variables – as one increases so too does the other. A negative correlation describes an *inverse* relationship – as one variable increases the other decreases. The numerical value of a correlation indicates the strength of the association. Consider the following correlations:

- $+0.85$ indicates that two variables are strongly and directly related to each other.
- $+0.4$ indicates that two variables are moderately and directly related to each other.
- $+0.02$ indicates that two variables are not related to each other (since the value is close to 0).
- -0.09 also indicates that two variables are not related to each other.
- -0.43 indicates that two variables are moderately and inversely related to each other.
- -0.84 indicates that two variables are strongly and inversely related to each other.

As in an experiment, we are still attempting to test a hypothesis and we may still need to be concerned with all of the same design issues. The main difference is that rather than developing and testing a hypothesis that predicts differences (e.g., that one group will score higher on some measure than another group), we test a hypothesis that predicts either a positive or a negative correlation (see the section in Chapter 3 on hypothesis testing). A second difference is that normally we take two measures from the same set of participants. So it could be said that most correlational studies are similar to repeated measures (in the sense that there is no random allocation of participants into groups, and that participants are measured by more than one variable).

We could conduct a correlational study that looks very much like an experiment. As an example, we could correlate the time taken to make simple judgements about pictures of faces with the ratings of how much each face is liked. Of course, we could equally conduct a correlational design that looks nothing like an experiment, for example by giving participants one personality measure and one ability scale to test for a correlation between them. In academic research it is often the case that a correlational analysis will be conducted within an experiment, i.e., it may be used to validate a dependent variable (for example, we may wish to test whether reaction time to some task and the number of errors made correlate before we are satisfied that reaction time is a valid dependent variable – very often we want participants to respond as quickly as they can in a study; if someone is trying to respond as quickly as they can we should expect more errors than if they are taking their time. Hence we should expect a negative correlation between time to react and the number of errors made).

Very often correlational approaches are used in conjunction with questionnaire designs, and especially in the development of a questionnaire (see later section on questionnaires). Furthermore, correlation can also be used to assess the reliability of a measure (see later section on reliability).

Correlation and causation

A relationship between two variables can be complex in terms of which causes which. Although we may find that two variables correlate highly with each other we are unable to say, without more information, which is the cause and which is the effect. It may be that a third variable causes both. For example, we may find that height correlates with verbal ability in a sample of children. Now we cannot say that an increase in height *causes* an increase in verbal ability, nor can we say that verbal ability causes an increase in height! However, a third variable, age, causes an increase in height and an increase in verbal ability. That said, when two variables correlate there may be a direct causal relationship between the two. For example, if reaction time to a task and the number of errors made were negatively correlated (i.e., the faster someone responds the more errors they make), it may be that the act of trying to respond very quickly increases the chances of making an error. In this sense, the faster someone responds *causes* more errors. The critical point is that we should not infer a causal relationship, however tempting it may be.

Correlational trends

It is worth making a point about strong correlations, since many students do not realise this point until they carry out their own correlational analyses. If we find a strong positive correlation between two variables, it follows that there is a *trend* for one variable to increase as another variable increases. This means that, although many of the data will follow this trend, there will be some cases where this will not be so. For example, even if we find a strong positive correlation between extraversion and assertiveness, we have not identified a rule that if one is extraverted then one must also be assertive – there will still be some cases where someone who scores high on extraversion will score low on assertiveness (and some cases where a participant has a low extraversion score and a high assertiveness score). The point is that a correlational analysis can uncover a trend rather than a rule about the relationship between two variables.

Questionnaires

Most questionnaires in psychology have been developed to measure either a particular *psychological characteristic*, such as general anxiety levels, leadership, attitudes to politicians, belief in the paranormal, and so on, or a *psychological ability*, such as verbal intelligence, numerical intelligence, spatial ability, and so on. These questionnaires (also known as *inventories* or *scales*) consist of a collection of questions (or *items*; say between 12 and 100). When a questionnaire has been completed it is then possible to total the scores for each question which gives a measure of the participant on the scale. In this method, it is assumed that people can be characterised by their scores on such scales.

In the development of a psychological scale, the investigator usually gives the questionnaire to many hundreds of participants from a wide variety of backgrounds or circumstances (depending on the nature of the scale). It is then possible to compare any new score with the scores of the large sample. For example, in the development of an anxiety scale, an investigator will give the questionnaire to a large number of people from as broad a range as possible, but will also include people who have been diagnosed with an anxiety disorder. The aim of this is to understand what constitutes a high score and what constitutes an average score, a process known as *standardisation*. In standardising a test, the test developer will publish the *norms* of the test or inventory. Norms are scores that indicate what high, average, and low scores are. For example, an inventory may produce scores between 1 and 20; a norm may indicate that only 5% of the population get a score above 18, or that 50% of the population obtain a score between 12 and 14. Norms may also be provided for specific groups, such as different age groups. Any subsequent participant taking the test can then be compared against the norms. In this way, norms help to give meaning to an individual score on the inventory.

There are at least four different ways of using a questionnaire in an investigation:

- A study in which scores on at least two different questionnaires undergo a correlational analysis.
- A comparison of the scores of two distinct groups of people on one questionnaire.
- An experiment in which the independent variable is decided by dividing participants into groups based on their score on a questionnaire.
- A study to develop a new psychological inventory.

A test of correlation between two questionnaires

In this method you give your participants two questionnaires and you apply a test of correlation. Clearly, the decision to do this has to be based on some theoretical position. For example, one theory of motivation might be that people who seek responsibility (people who prefer to take the initiative, and prefer a sense of freedom and personal control in situations) are essentially sensation-seekers (people who prefer to be in environments that stimulate them psychologically and physiologically). One way of testing this theory is to identify one questionnaire that measures individual responsibility (e.g., Franken, 1988) and one that measures sensation seeking (e.g., Zuckerman, 1979). Next, you apply both to the same sample of participants and do a test of correlation. Since the theory predicts a relationship, a strong positive correlation would be consistent with the theory; a very weak or close to zero correlation would provide evidence against the theory; and a strong negative correlation would not only provide evidence against the theory, it would also be very problematic for the theory (since it is directly opposite to the outcome predicted).

Although methodologically this appears to be a straightforward method, there are some practical problems with it. The first is identifying an appropriate questionnaire. Although there are many of these published, either (a) they are expensive to buy, or (b) you need to be trained in how to use them. Published questionnaires cannot be photocopied unless you receive direct permission from the publisher (it is worth asking them for this as it may well be granted for student use). However, the complete set of questions in many questionnaires can be found in the original research papers in which they were first introduced. So, if you have access to psychology journals then this is achievable. An alternative is to try a reputable website (for example, type the text "online psychological inventories" into a search engine such as Google) for tests that are free to use. However, you may need to make sure that the tests have been analysed for reliability and validity, otherwise the test may be inappropriate for a psychological investigation.

A second problem with this approach is satisfying your research criteria of (a) having a theory that predicts a relationship between two psychological characteristics, (b) that there exist two inventories that measure each characteristic, and (c) that you can get access to the measures. A short-cut is to work backwards from (c) to (a): find published inventories that you can use legally and that have reliability and validity measures, and then try to find a theory that predicts a relationship between them (however, make sure that there is meat to the prediction and that it is not a trivial or obvious one).

Comparing two groups on one questionnaire

In this method, you obtain two groups of participants (e.g., unskilled versus skilled workers, over 65s still in work versus over 65s who have given up work, and so on) and apply the same questionnaire. This is probably a more worthwhile exercise than testing for a correlation between two questionnaires because it is a better test of a theory. For example, one theory of anxiety might be that developmentally, anxiety develops in most children but that some children tend to *unlearn* their anxiety as adults, while others never lose it. This theory could be tested by applying the same anxiety inventory to young teenagers and to people in their late twenties. The prediction is that those in their late twenties will have lower anxiety scores than those in their early teens.

Another theoretically useful application of this method is to test the validity of an inventory. For example, the Eysenck Personality Questionnaire or EPQ (Eysenck & Eysenck, 1975) contains a measure of extraversion. According to Eysenck's theory of personality the extravert is low on arousal so seeks noise and excitement, while the introvert is over aroused and hence seeks peace and quiet. In the discussion below on validity, we will learn about how we can test a questionnaire for its validity (whether it measures what it claims to measure). So, if the above theoretical basis for the EPQ is correct then we should be able to identify at least one important difference between extraverts and introverts in their behaviour. One example might be whether a person smokes or not; we work on the assumption that smoking increases one's physiological and psychological arousal (which extroverts would seek) and that introverts are more likely to think about the dangers of smoking. In this case, we identify a sample of smokers and a sample of non-smokers (from the same population, i.e., so that they do not differ in other obvious ways). We apply the EPQ and predict that smokers will as a group score higher than non-smokers on extraversion. If the prediction is supported by the data then we have provided some validity for the theoretical basis of the EPQ.

Problems with this type of method include those mentioned in the previous section about obtaining a published questionnaire, and also the temptation to use an easy-to-find independent variable, such as sex. Many who use this method fall into the trap of comparing men and women on some measure, with the result that (a) there is precious little theoretical basis for the study, and/or (b) the results reveal no differences between men and women on the measure anyway! When using this method you must make sure that there is a sound theoretical reason for comparing the two groups on the measure you have chosen.

Using a questionnaire to divide your participants into two groups

In this approach, you have decided to conduct an experiment or an observation; however, your independent variable is simply those who score high on a measure and those who score low on a measure. One example of how this is used is in anxiety research, where participants who score high on an anxiety questionnaire are compared on some experimental task with those who score low on the questionnaire. As another example, you may wish to compare extraverts and introverts in an experiment, so you apply the EPQ to all participants first.

The division of participants into two groups can be done either by the "median-split" method or by referring to the published norms of the questionnaire.

- *The median-split.* In this method, you apply the questionnaire to your sample of participants and you obtain a score for each of them. The next stage is to calculate the median, or middle score. Then you classify anyone with a score above the median as the High Group (or experimental group) and anyone below the median as the Low Group (or control group). For example, suppose the scores obtained were 10, 10, 11, 12, 14, 17, 19, 19, and 20. The median is 14, so anyone scoring less than 14 is part of the Low Group and anyone scoring above 14 is part of the High Group. The participant who scored 14 can be classified as the Low Group since 14 is closer to the next lowest, 12, than to the next highest, 17; or alternatively, the data for this participant could be removed from any analysis, so that we have a good numerical distance between the scores of the two groups. The mean score of the Low Group is 10.75 (with the data point 14 removed from the analysis), and the mean score of the High Group is 18.75, so there is about an 8-point difference between the means of the two groups. The problem with this approach is that although it divides your sample in half, the value that separates the two groups (the median) is, to an extent, arbitrary – the median is likely to change each time a new sample of participants is taken. This is not a huge problem but it is something you should be aware of.

- *Consulting the norms.* The norms of an inventory can be found in either the manual that accompanies it or a published article on the inventory. The means and standard deviations of different groups based on age, sex, and occupation, are often provided. For example, if I were to apply the State-Trait Anxiety Inventory (STAI; Spielberger, 1983) to a sample of 16- to 18-year-old women students, I would then look up the mean State Anxiety score for this group and find that it is 35.2. Anyone scoring above this value becomes the High Group and anyone scoring below this value becomes the Low Group. The problem with this approach is that it is not guaranteed to divide your sample in half. You may need to recruit far more participants than you would otherwise wish, to ensure sufficient numbers fall into the two extremes.

While it is perfectly acceptable to divide your sample into two groups using either of these methods, you should be aware that this is not without its critics. The obvious criticism is that the questionnaire produces scores on a *continuous* scale – a score can take on any number within a range of values (scores on the STAI can vary from 20 to 80, so it is a 60-point scale) – but the method of division "converts" this into a *dichotomous* scale (a 2-point scale: Group 1 or Group 2). In doing so, two members of the same group can have very different scores yet be classified as the same group (e.g., a score of 20 and a score of 35 could both be considered as scores within the same group). Also, in creating two groups one ignores the range of scores that one has obtained and hence one is throwing away a lot of information. Therefore, another possibility is to attempt to correlate individual scores on an inventory with scores on a second task (that is, the dependent variable). Whichever method you choose, make sure that you discuss these limitations in your report.

A study to develop a new psychological inventory

You may decide to develop your own questionnaire, either because you cannot find or obtain the one you want, or because there isn't one and you fancy making up your own questions. Don't fall into the trap of thinking that this is an easy and straightforward thing to do. It can easily be more time consuming and involve more data analysis than an experiment, for the following reasons:

- The questions you create should use the same response scale.
- There should be a good number of "reversed" questions.
- You need to analyse the questionnaire for its reliability.

- You need to analyse its validity.
- You may need to apply it to test a theory.

Creating the questions

Normally, at the outset of the development of a questionnaire an investigator creates between 20 and 40 questions. The aim is to create a questionnaire that measures a *single* psychological concept or construct, such as anxiety level, risk-taking behaviour, extraversion, stress level, sociability, reactance, locus of control, and so on. Therefore, each question should ask about *one particular* concept. The idea is that you are developing a way of measuring someone on that concept – so if yours is a measure of sociability you do not want to introduce questions that ask about another issue, such as the person's stress level.

In creating 20 to 40 questions, you need first to decide on a response scale – how your participants are going to answer the questions. Responses need to be converted into numbers so that you can provide a measure for each participant on your scale. A response can either be consistent or inconsistent with your measure. So, for example, a "yes" response to the question: "Do you enjoy going to parties?" on a sociability scale is consistent with being "sociable" and scores 1, while a "no" response is inconsistent and scores 0. Common scales used are:

- *Yes/No.* Responses that are consistent with the theme of the questionnaire score 1; responses that are inconsistent score 0. The question should be worded so that only a yes or no response is appropriate.
- *Likert.* Responses are on a 5- or 7-point scale, such as "Strongly agree", "Agree Somewhat", "Neither Agree nor Disagree", "Disagree Somewhat", "Strongly Disagree". Each response can be scored 1 to 5, depending on how consistent it is with the theme. For example, suppose a different sociability scale asked "You should never wait for someone else to say hello before you say hello". The response "Strongly Agree" is consistent with being sociable, so it would score 5. The response "Agree somewhat" would score 4, "Neither Agree nor Disagree" would score 3, "Disagree Somewhat" would score 2, and "Strongly Disagree" would score 1. The "question" should be worded as a statement that someone can agree or disagree with (or feel neutral towards).
- *Other 4- or 5-point scales.* Apart from the agree/disagree format, you can use an always/often/sometimes/rarely/never format; a daily/weekly/monthly/occasionally/never format; a strongly like/like/neutral/dislike/strongly dislike format; or a not at all/

somewhat/moderately so/very much so format. This is not an exhaustive list of the scales used, and you can devise your own. The golden rule is to ensure that the wording of the questions you ask is appropriate for the response scale you use.

You should not mix the scales in one questionnaire – all 20 or 40 questions should be worded to fit the same response scale.

To generate questions, try to think about relevant characteristics or behaviours that are consistent with the theme of the questionnaire, and then try the opposite – think of behaviours that are inconsistent with the theme. For example, being sociable can involve not liking being alone, being constantly on the phone, enjoying going to parties, having many friends, being trustful of other people, and so on. Behaviours associated with not being sociable are: preferring to be on one's own rather than with others, avoiding eye contact, pretending not to see someone you know in the street, and so on. Each of these behaviours can be converted into a question with a suitable response scale.

Creating reversed questions

Psychologists use the term "response set" when a participant simply agrees with everything that is asked. In a questionnaire this means, for example, that the respondent ticks "Strongly Agree" to every question. So if all questions on a sociability scale were positively worded (i.e., a "Strongly Agree" response means they are sociable) then someone just agreeing for the sake of it would score unusually high.

To counteract this, reversed questions are introduced. For example, a positively worded question is "You should always go to parties you are invited to"; a reversed question would be "You should turn down invitations to parties from people you don't know very well". For a reversed question, a "Strongly Agree" response, in this example, would mean that they are not sociable. So for reversed questions the scoring is reversed, with "Strongly Agree" scoring 1, "Moderately Agree" scoring 2, "Neither Agree nor Disagree" scoring 3, "Moderately Disagree" scoring 4, and "Strongly Disagree" scoring 5. So, if you strongly disagree with the idea of turning down invitations to parties from people you don't know, then it is (most likely) because you are a sociable person. You do not need to have an even split in the number of normal and reversed questions, but should have at least one third of them in a reversed format.

In developing your own questionnaire, you will be expected to comment on the reliability of your questionnaire. A good suggestion is to conduct a split-half reliability analysis (see the next section on reliability and validity) and then offer ways in which you could test other forms of reliability in a future study. You will also be expected to comment on the validity of your measure. If you go on to use your questionnaire in one of the ways suggested above, you will auto-matically be doing something to test its validity (see the next section). If you plan to do a test of correlation with another questionnaire, you will be assessing its construct validity. If you plan to compare two groups on your questionnaire, you may be assessing its criterion-related validity. Finally, if you plan to use it to divide participants into two groups in an experiment then you will be testing its predictive validity – but note that the amount of work involved for an investiga-tion like this may be well beyond that expected from you.

Reliability and validity

In previous sections we have mentioned several times the problem of translating, or operationalising, a psychological concept into behaviour (e.g., the concept of memory into the act of recalling some-thing correctly or incorrectly; or developing a questionnaire to meas-ure anxiety). Two important issues regarding measurements are reli-ability and validity. You may not be expected to carry out tests of reliability and validity, but knowing about them may help you write about the limitations of your own study in the discussion section of your report.

The reliability of a measure refers to the extent to which the same measure produces the same measurement each time it is used on the same participant. In other words, if we were to assess how aggressive a child is using a particular measure, then that measurement should provide the same score or value each time we test the child. If we tested the same child twice but had two different scores or values then it is because the reliability of our measure is low.

How to increase reliability

Reliability is mostly used and assessed for in the development of questionnaires or inventories. Intelligence tests, attitude tests, and personality tests are examples of questionnaires and the Beck Anxiety Scale (Beck, Epstein, Brown & Steer 1988) is an inventory for measur-ing anxiety in adults. This is because tests that measure, say, reaction time have a high reliability because the same person is likely to score the same or similarly on more than one occasion. However, very often an inventory is "claiming" to be measuring something. For example, how do we really know that someone's score on Beck's Anxiety Scale would not fluctuate on a daily basis? To answer this question psychologists have developed several ways of testing for reliability.

Test–retest.   The obvious way to test for reliability is for the participant to take the same measurement on two occasions. If we assume that the psychological characteristic being measured is itself stable or unchangeable then our measure should produce the same or close to the same score or value. For example, if we developed a test of attitudes to politicians and we tested a sample of adults on Monday and then again on Wednesday, then a good measure would produce the same or very similar results (since we assume that attitudes do not change that quickly). If we obtained different results over the two days then we would conclude that the reliability of the measure is low. To increase reliability, we need to ensure that our measurement is accurate and that the same person would get the same "score" or behave in the same way if we tested them more than once.

Interitem reliability.   Interitem reliability refers to the ability of each question in a questionnaire to be asking about the same issue. A questionnaire in which questions are asking about different issues (e.g., "Do you often feel nervous for no obvious reason?" and "Do you prefer people with dark hair?") is unreliable. A questionnaire in which the questions are related (e.g., "Do you often feel nervous for no obvious reason?" and "Would you say that you're a bit of a worrier?") is reliable. To assess for interitem reliability, we do a correlational analysis on the responses to every possible pair of questions in the questionnaire. To increase reliability, items that have a low (close to zero) correlation with more than one other question are removed from the questionnaire.

Split-half reliability.   A simple way of testing for the reliability of a questionnaire is to divide it in half (e.g., first half of the questions and the second half of the questions, or the odd- and even-numbered questions), and test for a correlation between total scores on the two halves. High positive correlations imply high reliability; close to zero correlations imply low reliability. However, the problem with doing this is the fact that the way you divide the questionnaire into two is arbitrary – perhaps you would get different results depending on how you split it up. One solution would be to analyse every conceivable way of splitting the questionnaire in half, doing a correlation each time. You could then find the average correlation of all of the possible split halves. In fact, instead doing all of those analyses, there is a way of estimating the average correlation of all of the possible split halves, and it is called Cronbach's alpha. When this value is about 0.7 or above it is generally assumed that the reliability is high.

Validity

The validity of a measure (e.g., correct/incorrect recall) refers to the ability of a measure to capture accurately the psychological concept. For example, although recall is often used to infer the strength of a memory, research shows that recognising something is easier than recalling it. So, where one measure (e.g., recall) may indicate the absence of a memory, another measure (e.g., a test of recognition) may reveal its presence.

Face validity.   It may be the judgement of the researcher, colleagues, or of the participants themselves that the measure does indeed measure what it is intended to measure. This is known as face validity and is the judgement that "on the face of it" the measure appears to be valid and is not measuring something else. You should be aware, though, that something can appear valid but still have low validity, and also that something could appear invalid but have high validity.

Construct validity.   Up to now we have been using the term "psycho-logical concept" as a label that refers to such things as memory, aggression, and so on. Psychologists prefer the term *construct*. It refers to entities that have been studied and identified by psychologists, such as intelligence, personality, attitudes, long-term memory, spatial perception, and so on. A construct may not be observable directly but is inferred from behaviour. For example, we infer that the construct "memory" exists because people can remember some things and for-get other things. We can increase the validity of our measure by mak-ing sure at the outset that it is related to a measure that already exists. For example, if we used the measures of aggression in the previous example on a whole playground of children, we could obtain data on the number of aggressive acts for each child; we could then invite a teacher or parent to complete a standard published questionnaire on behalf of each child that measures his or her aggressiveness. For high construct validity, we should expect a high positive correlation between the two measures. The idea is that the construct you use must not be at odds with the existing literature. If a construct means one thing to one researcher and another thing by another researcher, then its construct validity is suspect.

Criterion-related validity.   Another way of assessing the validity of a measure is to assess it on a behavioural criterion. This means that we use one measure to make a prediction about another measure. For example, suppose we began our research on aggression in children the other way around – we have a set of completed questionnaires that gives us a score of aggressiveness for each child. In order to test for construct validity, we could observe, say, two of the highest-scoring children (i.e., those two rated as most aggressive) and two of the lowest-scoring children (i.e., those two rated as least aggressive) in the playground, using the observational coding scheme described above. The obvious prediction is that those rated as more aggressive will perform more aggressive acts than those rated as least aggressive. Another form of criterion-related validity is known as predictive validity – we assess the predictive power of a measure. The obvious example is that if A-level grades were able to predict degree classifications, the A levels would be said to have good predictive validity.

Surveys

A survey design is not to be confused with a questionnaire. In a questionnaire, we are measuring a particular thing about a person, such an aspect of their personality or a particular attitude, and there is only one response scale and one measure. In a survey we are attempting to describe opinions or behaviours on a broader range of issues (although typically focusing on one theme), and there are many response scales and many measures.

In a survey, we have greater freedom in choosing the questions: some can be of the yes/no format, while others can be based on a 3-point scale, and others still based on a 7-point scale. The aim is not to produce a single measure but rather several measures.

Cross-sectional designs

Most surveys are conducted on more than one group of participants at the same time. This way it is possible to compare, say, different age groups or different occupations on their views. Analysis of responses can reveal important differences between the groups. For example, questions about pension schemes given to young, middle-aged, and retired people are likely to reveal important differences in their attitudes towards having a private pension.

Longitudinal designs

A survey can be applied to the same sample of participants at two points in time, such as before and after an important event or simply just after the passage of time, to note changes in behaviour. Some examples might include a survey about crime and punishment before and after watching a TV programme about street crime, a survey of attitudes towards the Prime Minister before and after a general election, or even attitudes towards the study of psychology in the first and final weeks of the course!

In a survey the analysis usually involves simply comparing the responses between groups to key questions by presenting tables of the means and by plotting them on a graph. However, this can only be done with forced-choice responses, where the respondent ticks their favoured option for each question. It is also possible, though, to use open-ended questions (where the respondent supplies their own textual or verbal response) but it is not so easy to analyse these. An example of an open-ended question might be "In what way do you think your feelings towards the Prime Minister have changed now that you know the result of the general election?" However, it may be possible to categorise responses that are similar in some way and count the number of responses that fit in each category. The problem with doing this is that it tends to be subjective (a different investigator might classify them differently).

An important point in doing a survey is to remember that it is fruitless just to pick a topic of interest and ask a set of fascinating questions; your survey needs to be based on the idea of testing a theory. You should ask yourself: Can my survey provide support for a particular theory? Or you could ask yourself: Can my survey provide evidence that contradicts a particular theory? Since in general surveys are not the most scientific method for testing a theory, you should give a great deal of thought to these questions before choosing this method.

Observational designs

As with an experiment, the main aim of an observation is to test a hypothesis. It can be a preferred method over an experiment if the behaviour to be observed is more complex than can be studied in a laboratory, and when the investigator wishes to take measurements of behaviour that is more naturally occurring and less controlled by the constraints of the lab experiment.

Naturalistic observations

With a naturalistic observation, there is no interference or intervention by the experimenter. For example, a researcher may visit a mother and toddler group and observe child–parent interactions. Naturalistic observation is probably the purest form of observation and is akin to the way animals are studied in their natural habitat.

Participant observations

The problem with a naturalistic observation is that the investigator may be limited in the kinds of information that could be obtained. For example, since they do not interfere in the situation, they cannot ask questions. If they did ask questions, those being observed would realise that they are investigators and may then act differently (known as *reactivity*). With a participant observation, the investigator acts covertly (a disguised observation) and becomes a member of the group or situation. By doing this he or she may be able to uncover more information about the activities that are going on. The main problem with this type of observation is that the investigator is in danger of affecting the group in an important way or helping to make decisions for the group. There is also the ethical problem of not obtaining informed consent from participants who are unaware that they are being observed.

Contrived observations

Rather than observe people in their natural surroundings where the investigator has little control over the situation, a contrived observation is carried out in a pre-arranged location, such as a psychology lab. Often the investigator may be unseen by the participants, by viewing the activities through a one-way mirror.

The measurement issue: Inferring something psychological from behaviour

Whereas in an experiment the task is contrived by the experimenter and the set of responses required is also fixed, in an observation, the problem arises as to which behaviours to observe and how to measure them.

The main determinant of what it is you wish to measure is the theory you are aiming to test. There are two general methods of recording data:

- *Unstructured recording.* In this method you record as much relevant information as you can. In presenting your records, you describe the behaviours and offer interpretations of them. This is the method that Piaget used to develop his theories of cognitive and moral development in children.

- *Structured recording.* This is the most popular method and the one I recommend for your coursework. It is where you look out for specific acts or actions and you note their occurrence.

Structured recording

We will describe the method through an example. Suppose you wish to record the level of aggression displayed by child X and child Y in the playground.

- First, identify the "target behaviours", namely, those behaviours that you are interested in. In this example, it is any act of aggression.
- Second, you need a clear operational definition – that is, you need to be clear about which behaviours can be classified as aggressive and which behaviours could be interpreted in other ways. For example, you should list those behaviours that are clearly aggressive, such as punching, kicking, and throwing something at another child. You then need to think about behaviours that could be seen as aggressive or as something else. For example, shouting could be counted as an aggressive act, yet if the child is at some distance from another child or is playing tag, then this shouting may not be regarded as aggressive. If you do include such behaviours you should be clear about the conditions under which they should be counted as target behaviours.
- Third, you need to devise a scoring code. Suppose we have decided to record punching, kicking, and throwing something (other than a ball) at another child as our target behaviours. We could record behaviour in several ways, a tally sheet, a textual description, the duration of the behaviour, and the temporal order of behaviour.

Tally sheet.   We create a tally sheet for each behaviour on which we record the number of times it has occurred (the frequency of the behaviour). Make a mark for each occurrence and group the marks into units of five, for ease of counting, if you expect the number to be high (see Figure 4.3). You can then use the total for each behaviour and each child for your data analysis – you could compare child X with child Y on each of the behaviours. Alternatively, you could add up the total behaviours for each participant and compare child X and child Y on the total number of aggressive acts performed.

Figure 4.3. Example of a tally sheet used during an observation.

	Child X	Child Y
Punched	JHT III	III
Kicked	III	I
Threw	JHT JHT II	II

Duration of the behaviour. An alternative to just recording behavioural frequency is to record the duration, say in seconds. It is still possible to record the frequency by making a note of the duration of the behaviour each time, so that you may have, say, 5, 3, 1, 3 as four separate acts lasting a total of 12 seconds.

Temporal order. The above recordings do not take into account the order in which the behaviours occurred. For example, we would not know which child issued the first punch. Recording temporal order requires a different type of coding. In our example, you would write whether X or Y acted, which of the three acts they performed, and for how long. You would do this for each time one of the three acts of aggression was performed by X and Y. As you can imagine, this is not an easy task, and it is why investigators often videotape the situation so that they may score the behaviours using a video player, where the action can be paused, rewound, etc. Taping is often used when studying social interaction between three or more participants.

Rating scales. Another useful measure is to record not only when a behaviour occurred and for how long, but also its intensity. For example, X may tap Y on the face three times, and Y may respond with one forceful blow to X's face. By only recording frequency, the data suggests that X hit Y three times, but Y hit X only once. You could apply a rating scale for each behaviour, such as a scale of 1 to 5, where 1 is a small tap and 5 is a very hard blow. This way X will score 3 and Y will score 5. Of course, this is only useful if the target behaviours are not happening in quick succession (unless you choose to videotape the situation).

Interbehaviour latency. Another aspect of behaviour that an investigator may be interested in is the time between acts. So, for example, you may choose to record the time between a punch and a kick in order to describe in the data whether they tend to occur together.

Textual description. In addition to assigning numbers to behaviour, you could also record behaviour textually (e.g., "X hit Y directly in the face and with force"). You may wish to record unusual behaviours or incidents as text so that you could refer to them when reporting your numerical data (e.g., "Although X hit Y more frequently, on the occasion when Y hit X it was done with unusually strong force").

The type of coding you use is mainly dependent on the theoretical issue you are addressing. It also depends on whether it is possible to represent a psychological concept (such as aggression) through single acts of behaviour (e.g., punching). It also depends on how feasible it is to record target behaviours.

Content analysis

Content analysis has been used in a broad range of areas, from sociological studies to market research, and of course in psychology. It is based on the analysis of text taken from books, newspapers, magazines, journals, as well as transcribed conversations or speeches. The approach can be used to identify the intentions of the originator of the text, as well as their style of communication. It can also be used to identify a range of psychological or emotional states of a person. There are two main types of content analysis: conceptual analysis and relational analysis. I suggest that relational analysis may be far too complex for a student investigation, especially at introductory level, so we will only examine conceptual analysis here. In conceptual analysis, the aim is to identify the frequency of specific target words or concepts. As an example, one might select (at random) half a dozen pages from an autobiography, searching for key words that relate to the author receiving praise. The aim is then to keep a tally of the different words used that relate to the concept and how many times each word is used.

In determining whether a word qualifies to be included in the count, you could list relevant words in advance or you could use more than one person to do the coding so that you remove at least some subjectivity.

As with all other methods in psychology, you begin by asking a theoretical question. For example, suppose you wished to test Lewinsohn's (1974) theory of depression, which is that depression often begins as a result of receiving low levels of reinforcement (praise, support, compliments, and so on). You could test this theory by analysing the autobiographies of two famous people, where one of them had a known history of depression, and the other had no known depression. The theory would predict that since the depressed person has received less reinforcement than the non-depressed person, there should be fewer references to reinforcement in the depressed autobiography than in the non-depressed auto-biography. By comparing the frequency with which they use words associated with receiving reinforcement, it would be possible to show whether the depressed autobiography did indeed contain *fewer* of these words than the non-depressed autobiography. Of course, there are problems with drawing conclusions from such a study, but this gives you some idea of how to use content analysis in your investigation.

In terms of how many concepts or words to code for, there is no golden rule, and you can even code for word pairs or phrases. The key thing to remember is that ultimately you are coding for *concepts* used in the text. In doing the coding it may be that phrases are encountered that are not part of the original coding scheme but appear to be consistent with the concept being searched for. In this case, you can modify your coding scheme as you read the text. For example, you can code for words that imply a lack of praise, even when the terms praise, reward, compliment are not explicitly used. The precise coding method used (i.e., how you decided whether to count a concept as present) should be detailed in the procedure section of your report (these are known as translation rules). Once the coding is done for both texts, in this example, one can then make numerical comparisons between them, such as showing the frequency of the concept in both texts as a graph.

In terms of the validity of the analysis, this applies during the coding process where it is the reader's interpretation that is important, and this is a subjective thing. Two people may code very differently. Validity is also an issue when drawing conclusions from the analysis – that is, does the increased frequency of the concept "lack of reinforcement" in one selected text over another selected text, say, really mean that the author became depressed as a result of low levels of reinforcement? It is certainly not clear-cut, there are many other ways in which the two texts may differ and we may not be linking those with depression. Finally, although we attempt to draw generalisations (e.g., that most people would become depressed without reinforcement), their validity is also questionable and the best we may be able to say is that they are just consistent with the theory we are testing.

Content analysis is useful for looking directly at communication between people, and provides for a quantitative analysis. It is also an unobtrusive method of research since participants are not recruited or required to follow an experimental procedure or be interviewed. However, it is possible to create your own text to analyse by, for example, tape-recording conversations between pairs of people. The problem with content analysis is that it can be very time consuming on a practical level. On a theoretical level the conclusions drawn from an analysis may be too broad and imprecise to be able to test a theory in detail, and the analysis also ignores the context in which the conversation or text was carried out or created.

The following example is used to illustrate how content analysis can be used in an investigation. The study focuses on the use of text messaging and asks whether messages employ linguistic codes that non-text message users would not be able to understand, and whether text messaging is used as a replacement for face-to-face contact in a relationship.

An example: "Generation txt?"

Consider the study by Thurlow and Brown (2003) on use of text messaging or SMS (short-messaging services) in young adults. The authors state that there is little theoretical backdrop to the study because text messaging has been little studied. However, there exists a popular belief that text messages use language in new and novel ways and that they may come to replace face-to-face contact. So the study is set up to ask (a) what text messages are used for and (b) how different from conventional language are the messages.

The sample consisted of 135 students who provided a total of 544 messages that they had received in the previous week.

The results show very little evidence for the use of "letter–number homophones" (e.g., *GR8* for *Great*), and about 20% of the words were in an abbreviated form. Only 39 emotional expressions (emoticons) were used, e.g., ;), and many words were spelt phonetically.

Message categories

The following message orientation categories were found:

- *Information* (22%). A message sent to seek or to give practical or personal information.
- *Arrangements* (24%). A message sent to meet socially or discuss plans to meet up.
- *Salutation* (17%). A message sent as a greeting.
- *Friendship maintenance* (23%). A message sent to apologise, congratulate, or say thank you.
- *Romance* (9%). Messages that expressed love and intimacy.
- *Sex* (3%). Messages sent of a sexual nature.
- *Chain message* (2%). A message in the form of a joke or limerick sent from messenger to messenger.

The following themes were found:

- *Friendship work.* Text messages are used to maintain social relationships and are used alongside face-to-face interactions rather than replacing them.
- *Humour.* Text messages contain humour, which subserves the role of maintaining friendships and intimacies.
- *Chain messages.* These are often sent as sort of "gift", which is a way of social bonding.
- *Sex and flirting.* Text messages are used to flirt in a semi-anonymous way, i.e., although the receiver knows who the sender is, the physical distance, and the distance created by communicating in text, can encourage people to say what they would not say face-to-face.
- *Hyper-coordination.* Young people use SMS to keep in "perpetual contact" with their friends.
- *Co-presence and subversion.* SMS are often used when both sender and receiver are in each other's presence, often to deliver secret messages.

The author concludes that text messaging is used as part of social interaction and to maintain relationships but certainly not to replace them. Second, the linguistic codes used in text messaging resemble normal language use but with additional features (e.g., use of symbols and emoticons). There is little evidence of "subtraction", i.e., omitting to use punctuation.

This example demonstrates how content analysis can be used to test a hypothesis. The logic is to search for content whose frequency can be measured, gather evidence for or against the theory, and then weigh up the theory based on the evidence.

Data analysis 5

What is this chapter about?

Once you have gathered data from your participants, you will need to do work on the raw numbers to prepare them for analysis. You are not required to present the raw data in your results section but you are required to present summary data, including a table or tables to display the data and a graph or graphs to show your summary data visually. In this chapter we will look at the data collected in a quantitative investigation and how to calculate descriptive statistics, such as measures of central tendency and measures of dispersion. The chapter also shows you how to present your summary data in tables and graphs, and how to create a suitable table in Word® and various kinds of graphs in Excel®. Finally, you are given advice on how to comment on the data, tables, and graphs that you have presented.

Collating the data

In many cases, an investigation will comprise two groups of participants, or the same participants carrying out two different tasks. Each participant is likely to have undergone several trials on one or more tasks. You need to begin to collate the data into a form from which you can calculate group means and other statistics.

The first task is to separate the data according to the experimental and control groups or conditions. Second, for each participant, you should obtain his or her mean score or their total score, whichever is more appropriate. If using repeated measures you need to obtain, for each participant, their mean score (or total score) on the two tasks. The mean score is used when the task produces a continuous value, i.e., a number that has a minimum and a maximum and can take on any value in between. A good example is reaction time, and if you had 10 trials in each condition, you would calculate the mean reaction time for each participant for each condition.

Total scores are used when the task produces a very small range of values, such as 0 or 1. A good example is whether the answer on a trial is correct (and scores 1) or incorrect (and scores 0). If you had 10 trials of this type of task then you simply add up the number of errors. Alternatively, you could add up the number correct. You do this for each participant in each condition. Note that if the task can be done either correctly or incorrectly, you only need to count up the number of errors *or* the number correct, since the one value will always be dependent on the other (unless there are missing data).

If you intend to look at correlations between two variables (e.g., two different personality measures), you only need to provide two scores for each participant (e.g., their total score for questionnaire 1 and their total score for questionnaire 2).

Missing data

You should ensure that the means or total are calculated in the same way for each participant. This means that you need to think about how to deal with any missing data if there are any. For example, there may have been 10 trials and you are counting up the total number of trials for which a correct response has been made. One participant may have been distracted for one trial, and have only therefore been subjected to 9 trials. They may have 6 correct and 3 incorrect. Since they may or may not have got the missing trial correct (we will never know), we need to provide an appropriate score for them. We could do this by calculating a percentage correct score for each participant. In this example, 6 correct out of 9 would give them 66.7%. Similarly, we would convert the scores of other participants who did not miss any trials as percentages, so 6 out of 10 would give them a score of 60%.

Missing data are particularly problematic for questionnaires, especially those that produce a measure of some aspect of personality or attitude. This can happen when a participant unwittingly misses a question, deliberately misses a question they do not want to answer (and remember they are entitled to do this under the ethical code of conduct), or provides a "new" answer (e.g., writes *don't know* when the options are only *yes* or *no*). You have several options. The first is to remove all the data for a participant with missing data from any analysis. In effect, you treat them as though they never took part (except you say that you are doing this in your report). A second option is to fill in the blanks with a number that reflects a typical response, such as the mode or average response for that participant. So if the range of responses is, say, 1 to 5, and the mean response of their remaining data is 3.8, you enter 3.8 for the missing value. Alternatively, if the modal response has been 4, you could enter 4 for the missing value. In the case of a don't know response when a yes or no response is required, if yes scores 1 and no scores 0, then you could fill in the missing value with 0.5. Whichever method you choose, you should try to adopt the most sensible and unbiased approach, and you should always state clearly how you have treated cases of missing data.

Calculating summary information

You should be aware that in the results section, your intention should be to provide the reader with a summary of the data you have obtained. Normally, raw data are not presented in the results section and this is because it is standard practice to provide the reader with a "feel" for the data you have collected – the results should give a clear overall indication of the "shape" of the data you have collected. This means that you should present summary statistics as tables and graphs, as well as in the text.

How to calculate measures of central tendency

The mean

As discussed above, for each participant you may wish to calculate his or her *mean* score for each condition. Suppose a participant undergoes 9 trials in one condition, and their data look like this:

3, 4, 3, 5, 3, 3, 4, 5, 3

The mean is simply the numeric average of these scores:

(The 9 scores added together) ÷ 9

In this example, the mean is calculated as 33/9, which is 3.67. Note that the actual value on my calculator was 3.6666666; however, it is customary to round values to two or three decimal places, as appropriate.

Once the mean for each participant has been calculated, the next stage is to calculate summary data. In most investigations the mean of each condition is presented. However, it is not uncommon to report the mode or the median scores. The mean, say for condition 1, is its numeric average and is calculated by:

(The total scores for all participants in condition 1) ÷ (The number of participants in condition 1)

Suppose condition 1 produced the following data:

3, 3, 4, 3, 5, 3, 4, 4, 2, 3

The mean would be calculated as 3.4.

The mode and median

The mode is the most commonly occurring score, and in the above example would be 3 (since there are five of them, and only three 4s, one 5, and one 2). The median, which is the middle score, would be calculated first by reordering the numbers from low to high:

2, 3, 3, 3, 3, 3, 4, 4, 4, 5

Second, find the mid-point. In this case it is between the fourth 3 and the last 3. Since both numbers either side of this mid-point are the same, the median is 3. However, if both numbers were different, say 3 and 4, then the median would be the average of the two numbers, e.g., 3.5. Where there is an odd number of participants, the middle point will not be between two numbers but will actually be a number, as in the following:

3, 3, 3, 3, 3, 4, 4, 4, 5

There are nine scores and the middle score is the last 3, so the median is 3.

Relative advantages and disadvantages of the mean, mode, and median

The mean is most commonly used (where possible) since it represents the true central tendency of the set of scores. However, the mean is sensitive to outliers, that is, unusually high or low scores. So if most values were 3, 4, or 5, and you had one 12 among them, then the mean would be inflated and perhaps not be truly representative of the set of scores. Another disadvantage of the mean is that it can produce a value that did not occur in the sample (in the first example, the mean was 3.67, yet there was no single score at that value) or an impossible value (such as a report that says couples have on average 2.5 children or that the average shoe size is 8.56). The mode has the advantage that it is less affected by outliers than the mean. In addition, the mode shows the most important value in a set of scores. However, unlike the mean, the mode is less affected by other values in the sample. For example, it is possible to have a skewed sample (where there are numerous scores above the mode and only a few below it – an example of a negatively skewed distribution) but this is not reflected in the modal value. The median, which is the middle score, gives another indication of the central tendency of a set of scores, and is less sensitive to skewed data. A problem with both the median and the mode is that they can be quite unrepresentative of a sample if the sample size is small.

How to calculate measures of spread or variability

The range and standard deviation

Although a value such as the mean gives an indication of the central values of a sample of scores, it does not provide information regarding the range of scores obtained. For this reason it is customary, where possible, to provide a measure of the spread of the scores. The range is simply the minimum value and the maximum value (e.g., "The scores ranged between 2 and 5") and the numeric difference between the two, in this case 5 – 2, so the range is 3. By far the most commonly used measure of spread is the standard deviation or SD. The SD cannot be easily defined in words, and for a good understanding we need to look at a numerical example. You have my sympathy if you strongly dislike statistics, but read slowly and carefully. Although the calculation might appear rather complex, it is a very useful value to understand and to present in your results. The SD is calculated the following way:

1. Calculate the mean value of a sample (and call it M).
2. For each score in the sample find the numeric difference between the score and M, and then square that value.
3. Add all of the squared values and divide the total by the number of scores in the sample (called N) less 1 (i.e., N – 1). Call this number V.
4. Find the square root of V.

For the following set of scores: 3, 3, 4, 3, 5, 3, 4, 4, 2, 3, the steps are:

1. The mean is 3.4, so M = 3.4.
2. $(3 - 3.4)^2 = 0.16$
   $(3 - 3.4)^2 = 0.16$
   $(4 - 3.4)^2 = 0.36$

Table 2. A Frequency Distribution of the Scores Obtained	
Score	Frequency
2	1
3	5
4	3
5	1

Table 5.2. Example of a tabulated frequency distribution.

11. Centre all of the text except the title text.
12. To make the table look more interesting I chose one of the automatic table formats that comes with Word. Select *Table* from the menu bar then *AutoFormat*. Choose a style that is clear and interesting but not one that is garish or too colourful.
13. If you make mistakes and things get messy it is often easier to delete the table and start again than to try to repair it!

Presenting the data as a tabulated frequency distribution

A frequency distribution is a way of describing the spread of scores visually. The term "frequency" is used to mean "how often". It shows the range of possible scores and the number of participants that had each score. In the example data used above (3, 3, 4, 3, 5, 3, 4, 4, 2, 3), we note that one participant scored 2, five participants scored 3, three scored 4, and one scored 5. We could present these data as a table (see Table 5.2).

Tables like this can be very useful for "eyeballing" the data to see where most of the scores lie. This type of distribution is useful when the range of scores is quite low, but less useful when the range is large. For larger samples therefore, a *grouped frequency distribution* can be used. For example, suppose you had the following sets of scores:

4, 7, 8, 8, 9, 10, 10, 10, 12, 13, 14, 15, 15, 15, 16, 18, 18, 19, 20, 20, 21, 22, 22, 22, 22, 22, 23, 23, 23, 24, 24, 24, 24, 25, 27, 28, 28, 29, 31, 32, 32, 32, 34, 37

Table 5.3. A grouped frequency distribution.

Rather than produce a simple frequency distribution, we could group the data and present them as a grouped frequency distribution (see Table 5.3). Although there are 25 different scores in the sample (and hence 25 rows of data would be required for a simple frequency distribution), we have reduced this to 7 by grouping the data in units of 5. The class interval is the range of values for each group or class. The relative frequency is simply the percentage frequency for each class. As you can see from the table, the class 19–23 is the most frequent, and the frequency reduces as the class interval moves further away from the central class.

Table 3. Frequency and Relative Frequency Distributions		
Class Interval	Frequency	Relative Frequency
4–8	4	9%
9–13	6	14%
14–18	7	16%
19–23	12	27%
24–28	8	18%
29–33	5	11%
34–38	2	5%
Total	44	

Presenting summary data in a graph using Microsoft Excel®

Graphs are excellent ways of displaying data so that the reader can see at a glance what the data look like. However, graphs that are inappropriate, overly colourful and "glamorous", or just unclear, have the opposite effect.

There are several useful types of graphs, each of which has a specific name in statistics. For each type, you are given instructions below as to how to create it in Microsoft Excel®. Although there are some very sophisticated software tools on the market for analysing data and presenting graphs, the graphing abilities of Excel are both easy to use and very powerful.

The bar chart of means

The most often used graph in psychology is the bar chart of the means. The reader can see immediately which mean is the higher or highest and from which group. In Excel, create the table below (Table 5.4) on a hypothetical study about the effects of a distractor on performing some task.

Next, select six cells of the table by moving the pointer to the first cell of row 1, clicking and holding down the mouse button while moving the pointer to the third row second column (which is the cell with the number 4.1 in it) and then releasing the button.

Click on the graph icon after an *AZ* symbol and before the *?* symbol. In the window that opens make sure that the *Chart type* is set to *Column* and click *Next >*. Click *Next >* again in the following window. In *Value (Y) axis* enter "Reaction Time (seconds)". Click on the label or tab that says *Legend* and uncheck *Show legend*. Click *Next >*, then click *Finish*.

A graph will appear in your worksheet. We can make further changes to enhance it visually. First, although the Y-axis is in bold face, the title is not. So, double-click the text "Graph 1. Bar chart of group means", click on the *Font* tab and under *Font style* click *Bold*. Click *OK*. The next feature we wish to change is the greyness of the background. Double-click on the grey background and a window

	Graph 1. Mean Reaction Time With or Without a Noisy Distraction
Task done with noisy distraction	3.4
Task done in silence	4.1

Table 5.4. Text entered into Excel.

titled *Format Plot Area* should appear. If not, close whatever window does appear, click off the graph somewhere, and then try again. Under the label *Area* check *None*, and click *OK*. There is one final feature that you may wish to change and this is to do with the use of colour. It is usual practice in academic psychology to present graphs that appear in reports in greyscale. This means that colour is avoided and replaced by different shades of grey. However, this does not apply to the introductory student level and is a matter of personal choice. In order to change the bars to a shade of grey (or to another colour), double-click on one of the bars and under the label *Area* click one of the shades of grey or a different colour. To insert the graph into your word-processed document, click once on the outer edge of the graph, click the right-hand button on the mouse once, and choose *Copy*. In your word-processed document, such as Word, go to the Edit menu and select *Paste Special . . .*, and select *Picture (Enhanced Metafile)*. The graph will be placed, probably over text, in your document. To make the text flow around the graph, move the mouse pointer over the graph, click the right-hand button once, and select *Format Picture*. Click the *Layout* tab and select *Square*. Do not try to resize the graph as the text may become too condensed and will look rather odd. The graph that you have created should look just like Graph 5.1 below.

The histogram

In the section above on creating tables to present the data, we introduced the frequency distribution. As an alternative (or addition) to presenting these data as a table, they can be presented graphically, as a histogram (see Graph 5.2). Often, graphic information is easier to grasp than tabulated information.

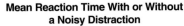

Mean Reaction Time With or Without a Noisy Distraction

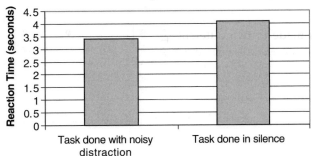

Graph 5.1.
Example of a graph created in Excel.

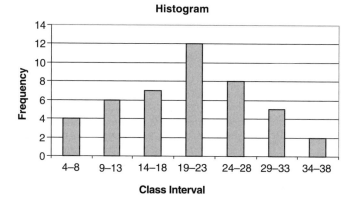

Graph 5.2.
Example of a
histogram created
in Excel.

If, instead of bars, Graph 5.2 had been composed of a line that joins the data points, then the graph is known as a frequency polygon. Both types of graph would convey the same information and in this case it is a matter of personal choice. However, a frequency polygon, or any line graph for that matter, cannot be used with ordinal or nominal data, only with interval or ratio. In other words, the use of a line indicates that the data are continuous (e.g., on a scale that has equal intervals). Scales that do not have equal intervals, such as a categorical scale, are not continuous and hence a line graph is inappropriate. The bar chart can be used for categorical data (a bar chart of the means is an example of this, as in Graph 5.1) as well as a pie chart. The histogram is created in a similar way to the bar chart, except that in the histogram there are more columns of data.

The scattergraph

For an analysis of correlation, the above graphs are unsuitable. Instead we can use a scattergraph, where we plot scores on one variable on the x-axis against scores on a second variable (see Graph 5.3).

Graph 5.3 shows the association between errors made in two different tasks. The pattern created by the data points can give a good visual representation of the nature of the association. Before we discuss such patterns, here's how Graph 5.3 was created. In Excel, create the data like those in Table 5.5. Next, highlight the data and the column

Graph 5.3.
Example of a
scattergraph
created in Excel.

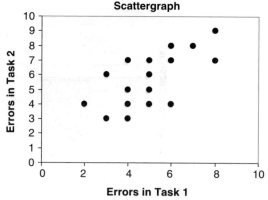

Errors in Task 1	Errors in Task 2
4	7
5	6
6	7
7	8
8	9
6	4
5	5
4	4
3	3
5	4
4	5
3	6
2	4
3	6
4	3
5	7
6	8
8	7

Table 5.5. Example data entered into Excel.

labels (move the mouse pointer to the first cell *Errors in Task 1*, click and hold the left-hand button on the mouse down, move the pointer to the last cell in the right containing the number 7, and then release the button).

Then click on the chart icon in the menu bar (or select *Insert* then *Chart* in the menu bar). Under *Chart type* select *XY (scatter)* then click *Next >* and then *Next >* again. In the *Titles* tab enter the title of your graph and in the *Legends* tab uncheck *Show legend*. Click *Next >* and the *Finish*. You can now edit the graph in the way we edited the bar chart.

The pie chart

The only other type of graph we have not mentioned so far that is commonly used to present data in psychology is the pie chart. This is suitable for displaying the responses to or frequencies of a number of categories, such as the different types of responses to an item in a survey. The "pie" is split into "slices", the size of which represents the frequency of responses for that category. For example, suppose we ran a survey on the types of investigations that students did for their psychology coursework. One of the questions we might devise is: "Which *one* of the following answers best describes how you presented the data visually? Bar chart, Histogram, Frequency polygon, Scattergraph, Pie chart, More than one of these, None". The data from this type of question, where the response is selected from a number of categories, are most suited to the pie chart (see Graph 5.4).

To create this pie chart in Excel, create a table of data with labels as with the previous examples, and select the *Chart* icon. This time, select *Pie* as *Chart type*, click *Next >* and then *Next >* again. Type in your *Chart title* and click the *Legend* tab. Uncheck *Show legend*. Click the *Data Labels* tab and select *Show label and percent*. Click *Finish*. To change the font size and style, double-click somewhere on the

Graph 5.4. Pie chart created in Excel.

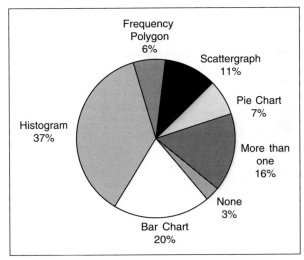

text. To change the colour area of a slice, or to make them different shades of grey, click on the chart, then click on the slice you want to change, pause for a second and then double-click on the slice. You can change its colour under the label *Area*.

A comment on the general presentation of graphs

When creating the above graphs, I played around with various charting features that are supplied with Excel, such as using patterns for bars or slices (or even pictures). It is also possible to create graphs that look three-dimensional. The masterpiece I created is shown as Graph 5.5 (in fact the graph itself was in full colour but is shown here in grey scale).

Compare this graph with Graph 5.2. Notice that they contain the same data and the same labels. Although Graph 5.5 looks "fancier" than Graph 5.2, most of its dressing conveys *no new information at all* (in fact, it is more difficult to read). A rule of thumb, then, is keep your graphs and tables simple, and do not make any change to them that does not convey more information, however fancy it looks. Colour is usually avoided because it doesn't photocopy (unless someone goes to the unnecessary expense of colour photocopying).

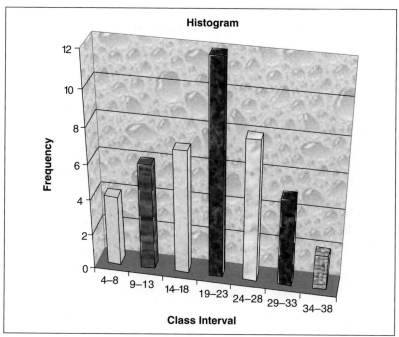

Graph 5.5. A graph produced by exploiting a number of the features in Excel's Chart Wizard.

Labelling graphs and tables

- *Title.* The title of a table or graph should begin with a number, such as "Table 1" or "Graph 1" and these should be consecutively numbered if there is more than one. The title should then give some indication of the variables used in the study, such as "The mean response times with and without noise in the background". In the case of a graph, you may like to add text about the kind of graph it is, so the full title might be "Graph 1. A bar chart showing the mean response times with and without noise in the background".
- *Axes.* In the case of a graph, there are two axes, the vertical axis (or the y-axis) and the horizontal axis (or x-axis). It is standard practice to label the vertical axis with the dependent variable, such as "Mean Reaction Time", and the horizontal axis with the two conditions or groups (the independent variable), such as "With Background Noise" and "Without Background Noise". Often students create their data (say, in Excel) using shortened or made-up words like "withno" and "withoutno" and then label their graphs with these pseudo-words. You will lose marks if you do not label your graphs correctly, using real words that indicate what the data actually represent.

Drawing inferences from the data

Remember that the immediate aim of an investigation is to test a hypothesis. Once you have calculated and presented the summary data you need to draw some conclusions about whether the data have provided support or otherwise for the hypothesis.

The requirements of inferential tests of significance

If you are required to use inferential tests, then any conclusions should await the outcome of that test (or tests) and you should only offer comments about whether the data *appear* to support the hypothesis. However, if you are *not* required to use inferential tests, then you can, indeed should, provide an appraisal of the data.

The hypothesis of your study is worded to provide a precise prediction about one (or both) of the following:

- Differences between two groups or conditions on some measure.
- Whether two variables are positively or negatively correlated.

In terms of differences, you can comment on which group has the higher mean, mode, or median, and whether this difference is in the same direction as the hypothesis. If they are in the same direction, then these data have provided support for the hypothesis, or if the values of two groups are very similar then the data fail to support the hypothesis. If, however, there is a difference but it is in the opposite direction, then this not only fails to support the hypothesis, it runs counter to the hypothesis (and will warrant some explanations as to why this may have been so). In addition, you can offer some conclusions about the spread of the scores from each condition (for example if you have plotted a histogram for each condition, describe how they are different or similar).

You follow a similar discussion if you are testing for a correlation. You can comment on the value of the correlation, and whether its sign is in the same direction as the hypothesis. If the hypothesis predicts a positive correlation and the data show a positive correlation, or if it predicts a negative correlation and the data reveal a negative correlation, then the data support the hypothesis. If there is no correlation then the data fail to support the hypothesis. If, however, there is a difference between the sign of the correlation between the hypothesis and what is obtained in the analysis, then this not only fails to support the hypothesis, it runs counter to the hypothesis (and will warrant some explanations as to why this may have been so). In addition, you can offer some conclusions about the pattern that emerges from the scattergraph (if you have provided one). For example, are there any outliers or are any scores clustered around the same values?

A point to note is that it is not *your* hypothesis, *your* results, or *your* data to which you should refer – you should adopt an impersonal stance in the results section. This may seem strange since it *was* you who devised the hypothesis, gathered the data, and analysed the results. However, an investigation is not a test of the author but of the theory that the investigation is aimed at testing. An investigation with data that do not support the hypothesis is not a *failure* in the sense that it was a worthless exercise, and it does not mean that the investigator has failed. It means that there are problems with the theory. Indeed, a study that fails to find support for a theory can be more informative than a study that supports a hypothesis. In sum, you should not in any way refer to the hypothesis or data as yours, and you should never feel that you or your study have failed if the data do not support the hypothesis.

If you are required to conduct inferential statistics, read the next chapter carefully.

Inferential statistics 6

What is this chapter about?

The specification you are following may require that you conduct inferential tests on your data (see Appendix 1). You also need to check whether the specification you are following requires you to do inferential statistics. While these can be laborious to calculate, their logic is relatively simple, and they are of great value in helping you to draw conclusions about your data. This chapter helps you decide on a suitable test, shows you how to calculate the statistics for the test, and guides you in understanding how to interpret the results and use them in your report.

The logic of the inferential test

Think of a number between one and ten

Suppose two groups of students (call them Group A and Group B, with 100 in each group) were asked to think of a number between 1 and 10. Suppose I added up the numbers given by Group A and divided this by 100. I would have the mean number generated by Group A. I then find the mean number for Group B.

Now, provided that both groups were asked the same question and in precisely the same way, and also generated their response in the same way (e.g., by writing it down on a blank piece of paper), there is no reason to believe that the mean of Group A should be much different from the mean of Group B. So, if the mean of Group A was 5.5 and the mean of Group B was 5.6, this kind of result would not differ from what was expected. Note that we would rarely expect exactly the same values.

Suppose I (the person analysing the data) was told that one of the following had occurred:

1. The students in *Group A* with dark hair were secretly instructed to produce their number between 7 and 10, or:

2. The students in *Group B* with dark hair were secretly instructed to produce their number between 7 and 10, or:
3. No student in either group was given instructions other than to produce a number between 1 and 10.

My task is to work out which one of these three possibilities was true. I do this by comparing the means of Group A and Group B. If the means were quite close (e.g., 5.5 versus 5.6) I would conclude (3), that there were no extra instructions given. However, if one group scored quite a bit higher than the other (e.g., 5.5 versus 7.8) then I would be tempted to conclude either (1) or (2) depending on which group had the higher mean.

Suppose, however, *by chance* Group A included five people whose favourite number is 9 and Group B included five people whose favourite number is 2. So, by chance Group A gets a higher mean than Group B and this has nothing to do with the instructions they were given. Suppose, in this case the means were quite close but one group was still a bit higher than the other, such as 6.2 versus 5.1, a difference of 1.1. This becomes a grey area for me, since I do not know whether 1.1 is sufficiently greater than what should be expected if the instructions were exactly the same.

This is precisely the problem faced when one looks at the data gathered in an experiment. Any difference between two means could be due to the independent variable or could be due to chance (caused by something else). Furthermore, while a difference of 2.5 between the two means implies that one group was given "special" instructions and the other was not, what should I conclude if the difference was 1.2 or 0.6, or 0.3? Where should I draw the line? One answer is: I haven't a clue! Another answer is: Use inferential statistics.

What does an inferential test tell us?

An inferential test can be devised to tell us whether to accept a difference as due to the independent variable (e.g., some students in Group A were given different instructions from Group B) or whether it was due to chance. We don't need to devise such a test ourselves – such statistical procedures have been devised on our behalf by statisticians.

An inferential statistical test tells us how likely it is that the differences or relationships data we have obtained, say from two groups, are due to chance or due to the independent variable. For the hypothesis to be supported, the test needs to tell us that the data are due to the independent variable. If it tells us the data are likely to have been due to chance then this would not support the hypothesis. This concept is known as *statistical significance* (see below). In our "think of a number between one and ten" example, we could apply an inferential test, and it would calculate the probability that the difference between the two means is due to chance or due to the independent variable.

In the following, we describe a number of commonly used tests with worked examples. However, there is no attempt to show you mathematically how and why each test works. I would estimate that probably only one in a hundred students would *completely* understand. In any case, you would not be expected to know this for any specification. The features of a test you would be expected to know are: (1) the rationale for the test, (2) the type of data that are relevant for the test, (3) the mechanics of how the test is calculated, and (4) how to interpret the result of the test.

Why we don't need to know the maths: How does a television work?

If you were asked how a television worked you might begin by saying that signals are beamed from a transmitter at the television company's studios, which are picked up by your aerial. You might then go on to say that the television receives this information and converts it to coloured points on the screen, and that it "paints" the screen with these points many times a second. You might go on to to mention that the points consist of mixtures of red, blue, and green, and you might know the precise number of dots on a screen and the precise screen refresh rate. However, unless you have majored in electronics, at some point your reply will stop short of a full and complete explanation. Somewhere there will be a leap of faith. You don't really have complete knowledge of how a television works; what you do have is partial knowledge of a television system. Similarly, in trying to understand inferential statistics, unless you are a pretty neat mathematician, at some point you will be compelled to make a leap of faith.

For these reasons I will not attempt what I might choose to call a "statistically violent" explanation of each test, but rather we will take a more pragmatic approach: how can I use them and learn how to describe them such that I can get a good grade in my psychology coursework? For those readers who feel comfortable with statistical violence, you might like to read Howell (1997).

In all of the specifications that prescribe the use of inferential statistics, not one says that you should use what are called *parametric* tests. In order to partially understand parametric tests you would need to know a little more about statistics than you would probably like to! For this reason, I would advise you to use one of the simpler *non-parametric* tests that are described in this chapter (all of the tests are non-parametric, except the two *t*-tests). Again, students who enjoy a bit of statistical violence can consult Howell (1997).

Hypothesis testing

The hypothesis and the null hypothesis

Up until now we have used the term "hypothesis" as the prediction that we are testing in an investigation. Its fuller term is the *experimental hypothesis* or the *alternative hypothesis*. There is also the null hypothesis, which has almost the opposite meaning. If a hypothesis predicts that

Group A will score higher than Group B on a task

then the null hypothesis predicts that

Group A *will not* score higher than Group B.

Note that all we have done is replace the word *will* with *will not*. When we wish to use inferential statistics to infer whether or not our hypothesis is true, we introduce the term *significantly* into the hypothesis and null hypothesis, like this:

Group A will score significantly higher than Group B on a task.

And for the null hypothesis:

Group A will not score significantly higher than Group B.

In practice, statistical tests have been devised to test whether the null hypothesis (i.e., a chance effect) is true.

Directional and nondirectional hypotheses

The above hypotheses and null hypotheses are examples of *directional hypotheses* because they stipulate a *direction* of the difference: that one specific group will score higher than the other group or that one specific group will not score higher than the other group. Directional hypotheses are chosen when such a prediction follows directly from a theory. For example, if I theorise that the reason why people eat is because they are hungry, then if I put hungry people and satiated people in a room together with lots of food, I would predict that hungry people will eat significantly more than will satiated people (and my null hypothesis would be that hungry people will not eat significantly more than will satiated people).

A nondirectional hypothesis is a prediction of a difference without stating the direction of the difference: the groups will have different scores, but which group has the higher score is not predicted. For example, suppose I read about a theory that a child is only naughty when it isn't getting positive attention. In order to develop the theory further, I may wish to compare middle-class and working-class caregivers in the amount of positive attention they give their children. One aspect of the theory states that working-class caregivers give more positive attention than do middle-class caregivers. However, a competing theory posits the opposite. When I devise an experiment or observation I am testing two theories and I do not have any expectation about the outcome. I therefore develop a nondirectional hypothesis, such as "Working-class caregivers and middle-class caregivers will give significantly different amounts of attention to their children" (although I would have to be clear about what was meant by "amounts" and how to measure it). My null hypothesis is then "Working-class caregivers and middle-class caregivers will not give significantly different amounts of attention to their children".

For reasons that are of a statistically violent nature, a directional hypothesis is also known as a one-tailed hypothesis, and a nondirectional hypothesis is also known as a two-tailed hypothesis.

Statistical significance

The inferential test is set up to test the null hypothesis. In fact, the test will calculate for us the *probability* that the null hypothesis is true. Although the test gives us probability as a numerical value, it can be interpreted qualitatively with terms such as "highly probable", "probable", "highly improbable". Note that if the null hypothesis is highly improbable then it follows that the only alternative, the experimental hypothesis, must be highly probable or "highly statistically significant".

Before continuing the discussion, it is important to note that the "traditional" way of calculating the statistical significance of a test involved the use of tables (some of which you will find in Appendix 2 of this book and in similar research methods books). Probabilities were not actually calculated, but the result you obtained was compared to "critical values" in a table. However, given that the computer is now commonplace, it is possible to calculate probabilities directly. In the discussion that follows we will talk about actual probability values, although these may not be accurately known if you use the "looking up the critical value in the table" method.

Inferential tests are tests of whether the hypothesis is highly statistically significant, statistically significant, or not statistically significant. To collate these terms for better understanding see Table 6.1.

There are a few things to notice about Table 6.1. First, the probability value is a number between 0 and 1. Second, a probability of 0 means that something is impossible and a probability of 1 means that something is a certainty and guaranteed to happen. The third thing to note is that the higher the value in the first column the more probable is the null hypothesis. The fourth thing to note is that I have drawn a heavy line above 0.06 and below 0.04. This is because the interpretation changes dramatically around this line. The line is actually set at 0.05 and is a standard value, known as *alpha*. Social scientists have chosen this value as a decision point about how to interpret the probability value obtained from an inferential test.

- *Anything below 0.05* (or equal to 0.05) is taken to mean that the null hypothesis (being improbable) is to be rejected. If the null hypothesis is rejected then the experimental hypothesis is accepted, and the result is said to be statistically significant.
- *Anything above 0.05* is taken to mean that the null hypothesis is now sufficiently probable, and is to be accepted. If the null hypothesis is

Probability that the null hypothesis is true	Interpretation of the truth of the null hypothesis	Interpretation of the result
0	Impossible	It has guaranteed significance
0.001	It is highly improbable	It is highly statistically significant
0.01	It is highly improbable	It is highly statistically significant
0.04	It is improbable	It is statistically significant
0.06	It is probable	It is not statistically significant
0.2	It is probable	It is not statistically significant
0.95	It is highly probable	It is not statistically significant
1.0	It is guaranteed	It is impossible

Table 6.1. Interpretation of the results of an inferential test.

accepted then the experimental hypothesis must be rejected, and the result is said to be statistically non-significant.

To remind you, the *probability that the null hypothesis is true* is what our test produces for us, and it is a number between 0 and 1. It is also known as a *p* value.

So why 0.05?

As stated above, alpha is set at 0.05, and it is a cut-off point for drawing a conclusion (or inference) about whether to accept or reject the null hypothesis. Remember that a *p* value of 0.05 is equivalent to a 5% probability or a 1 in 20 probability. You may be asking why 0.1 or 0.5 isn't used, or why 0.1234567 isn't used (it's a cute enough number!). The answer is rather disappointing for the purists among us. It was developed 80 years ago by a scientist named Fisher. As I understand it, Fisher, who was pretty handy at statistics and probability, did not arrive at this number through dozens of pages of abstract mathematics. No, he chose it because it seemed "about right":

> ... it is convenient to draw the line at about the level at which we can say: Either there is something in the treatment, or a coincidence has occurred such as does not occur more than once in twenty trials. ... Personally, the writer prefers to set a low standard of significance at the 5 per cent point, and ignore entirely all results which fail to reach this level.
>
> (Fisher, 1956, p. 504)

Ever since, psychologists and similar have been treating it as something to bow down to and as something to be humble about in its presence – a number that can make or break a theory.

More recently, psychologists have begun to consider values on the upper side of 0.05, such as 0.06 up to about 0.1, as "trends", meaning that it might be worth repeating the study with a slight change to the procedure to see if significance moves to below 0.05.

In sum, we obtain a *p* value from the inferential test, compare it to 0.05, and if it is less than 0.05 we reject the null hypothesis and accept the experimental hypothesis. If it is greater than 0.05, we accept the null hypothesis and reject the experimental hypothesis. If the *p* value is very low we make a note of this in the report, since it means that we have a highly statistically significant result.

Use Table 6.2 when attempting to draw conclusions from the

Table 6.2. The inference made from a given *p* value.

p value (always expressed as a decimal number)	Expressed as a less than one-in-something	Expressed as a percentage	Decision expressed as a comparison of alpha and the p value	Significance expressed qualitatively	Decision about the hypotheses
0.0006	Less than one-in-a thousand	0.06%	$p < 0.001$	Highly statistically significant	Reject null, Accept experimental
0.006	Less than one-in-a hundred	0.6%	$p < 0.01$	Highly statistically significant	Reject null, Accept experimental
0.01	One-in-a hundred	1%	$p < 0.01$	Highly statistically significant	Reject null, Accept experimental
0.04	One-in-twenty-five	4%	$p < 0.05$	Statistically significant	Reject null, Accept experimental
0.05	One-in-twenty	5%	$p \leq 0.05$	Marginally statistically significant	Reject null, Accept experimental
0.06	Six-in-a hundred	6%	$p > 0.05$	Just outside significance	Accept null, Reject experimental
0.1	One-in-ten	10%	$p > 0.05$	A trend towards significance	Accept null, Reject experimental
0.2	One-in-five	20%	$p > 0.05$	Not statistically significant	Accept null, Reject experimental
0.5	One-in-two	50%	$p > 0.05$	Not statistically significant	Accept null, Reject experimental
0.9	Nine-in-ten	90%	$p > 0.05$	Not statistically significant	Accept null, Reject experimental

inferential test you have used. First, note that anything from about 0.15 onwards is considered not statistically significant (in fact, a value of, say 0.2 is qualitatively the same as 0.9). Second, note the use of the term "not statistically significant" rather than the term "insignificant" (which means "of no importance at all" – and the result is very important for the study, at least).

Finally, before we leave this section you should be aware that you will be doing the calculations by hand. There are a few software packages that can do the calculations for you – indeed tests used in these packages calculate the p values for you. However, doing the test by hand does not provide you with a p value. Instead it provides you with something called a "test value". Using significance tables, you look up the test value to see if it is greater or less than a critical test value, to determine if it is statistically significant at a specific level, such as 0.05, 0.025, 0.01, and so on. There are further instructions on what this means for each test, below.

Which test? Choosing a test and justifying your choice

There are several different types of inferential tests, and the one you should use depends on a number of things, such as the *type of data* obtained in the study, whether a *repeated measures or independent measures* design was used, and whether the hypothesis predicts a *difference or an association*.

Data types
There are four different data types:

- *Nominal.* A nominal scale is one where *names* are used to categorise the data. Examples include: whether an error was made on one task or whether it was correct (e.g., the scale is *correct* or *incorrect*), the selection of a response from one of a number of options (such as left, centre, or right), categorising someone as part of one group or part of another group (e.g., conservatives and liberals), or determining how many items or numbers are greater or less than a specific value (e.g., the list: 87, 99, 121, 105, 76, 112 in terms of whether they are greater or less than 100 produces three less than 100, and three greater than 100). With nominal data one simply has a list of items and a number or count for each item.
- *Ordinal.* An ordinal scale is one where items can be placed in an ordered list. Examples include: ordering a list of pictures on the basis of how much they are liked (most liked, second most liked, third most liked, and so on until least liked), the order of the contestants in a race (first, second, third, fourth, and so on), or rearranging a list of numbers into the highest first (e.g., 4, 5, 3, 6, 5, 3, into the list 6, 5, 5, 4, 3, 3).
- *Interval.* An interval scale is one where there are a set of numbers that have an equal interval between them, such that the difference between 2 and 3 is the same quantity as the difference between 5

case condition 2 has scored higher than condition 1). If there is about the same number (give or take a handful) then the scores from the two groups do not differ significantly. The actual "handful" required is calculated in the test. It does this by use of "binomial probability" – this asks: if there are only two outcomes with N observations, what is the probability of obtaining S number of observations for the one outcome and N–S for the other outcome?

How do I calculate the sign test? Example data

- Step 1. Draw a table that allows you to compare the two scores from each participant (see Table 6.4).
- Step 2. Taking each participant in turn, if their score on condition 1 is higher than their score on condition 2 then insert + in the row below, otherwise if their score on condition 1 is lower than their score on condition 2 then enter –. If the two scores are the same leave it blank.
- Step 3. Count up the number of +s, the number of –s.
- Step 4. Identify which is the lower of these two values and call it S.
- Step 5. Count up the number of participants who have *either + or –* (and no blank) and call it N.
- Step 6. Look up the statistics table Appendix 2a. Find the row corresponding to the N you have obtained. Next, identify the column for the S you have obtained. The values in this table show *actual significance values* (and based on whether you have a one-tailed or two-tailed hypothesis). If the value is less than 0.05 then the difference is statistically significant.

Worked example

Steps 1 and 2. See Table 6.4.
Step 3. 6 +s and 2 –s.
Step 4. S = 2.
Step 5. N = 8.
Step 6. The value found is 0.144. The difference is not statistically significant.

Participant	1	2	3	4	5	6	7	8	9
Scores on condition 1	18	14	17	15	18	19	23	15	16
Scores on condition 2	15	13	14	16	14	11	16	16	16
Difference	+	+	+	–	+	+	+	–	0

Table 6.4. Example data for the sign test.

How do I report the result?

The above result is reported as:

> According to the sign test, the difference between the scores from the two conditions is not statistically significant at the 5% level. For N = 8 the actual probability for S = 2 is 0.144 ($p > 0.05$, one-tailed). Therefore, there is a greater than 5% probability that the observed difference is due to chance. The null hypothesis is accepted and the experimental hypothesis is rejected.

If we had obtained a value of S as 1 then the result would be reported as:

> According to the sign test, the difference between the scores from the two conditions is statistically significant at the 5% level. For N = 8 the actual probability for S = 1 is 0.035 ($p < 0.05$, one-tailed). Therefore, there is a less than 5% probability that the observed difference is due to chance. Since the difference is statistically significant, and since the mean of condition 1 is higher than the mean of condition 2, the null hypothesis is rejected and the experimental hypothesis is accepted.

You may note that we have found the actual p values for this test; see the section "On reporting p values" to find out more about this.

Test of difference 2: The Wilcoxon matched-pairs signed ranks test

When should I use this test?

This test is used when the data are ordinal or interval, when you are looking to test for differences, when your design is repeated measures, and when you want a more powerful test than the sign test. (Note that this test is *not* to be confused with the Wilcoxon rank sum test for two independent samples.)

What is the logic behind the test?

For each pair of scores, you find the numeric difference. These are then ranked according to their absolute values (i.e., regardless of which condition produced the higher value) – this means assigning 1 to the smallest number, 2 to the next smallest number and so on. These are their ranked values. The signs are then added to the ranked values (for each pair, add + if condition 1 is higher than condition 2, or − if condition 2 is higher than condition 1). The ranked values of the +s are summed, and the ranked values of the −s are summed. If the two conditions differ significantly, then there should be a larger rank sum for one condition over the other. If the rank sums are about the same (more or less) then the scores from the two groups do not differ significantly. The actual "more or less" required is calculated in the test.

How do I calculate the Wilcoxon matched-pairs signed ranks test? Example data

- Step 1. Draw a table that allows you to compare the two scores from each participant (see Table 6.5).
- Step 2. Taking each participant in turn, write down the numeric difference, including the sign: if their score on condition 1 is higher than their score on condition 2 then insert + in the row below, otherwise if their score on condition 1 is lower than their score on condition 2 then enter −. If the two scores are the same, leave it blank.
- Step 3. Rank the numbers by ignoring the sign, i.e., assign 1 to the lowest score (regardless of the sign of the numbers) and 2 to the next lowest and so on. If two items have the same value then "share" the rank scores. In the above example, participants 2, 4, and 8 each have a difference of 1, and the next three rank values should have been 2, 3, and 4; so they share the rank value $(2 + 3 + 4)/3 = 3$.
- Step 4. Insert the sign to the rank values, based on the difference score.
- Step 5. Add up the values of the positive ranks and call it T+.
- Step 6. Add up the values of the negative ranks and call it T−.
- Step 7. Add up the number of pairs (or participants) and call it N.
- Step 8. Identify which is the smaller of the two values T+ or T−.
- Step 9. Look up the statistics table Appendix 2b. Find the row corresponding to the N you have obtained. Beginning with the

Table 6.5. Example data for the Wilcoxon matched-pairs signed ranks test.

Participant	1	2	3	4	5	6	7	8	9
Scores on condition 1	18	14	17	15	18	19	23	15	16
Scores on condition 2	15	13	14	16	14	11	16	16	16
Difference score	+3	+1	+3	−1	+4	+8	+7	−1	0
Rank	5.5	3	5.5	3	7	9	8	3	1
Signed Rank	+5.5	+3	+5.5	−3	+7	+9	+8	−3	0

right-most column, identify whether the T you have obtained (ignoring its sign) is less than or equal to the value in the row. If you have found a value that is greater than the value of T you have obtained, look at the column heading for the significance level (based on a one- or two-tailed hypothesis). If no value is found then the difference is not statistically significant.

Worked example

Steps 1 to 4. See Table 6.5.
Step 5. $T+ = 5.5 + 3 + 5.5 + 7 + 9 + 8 = 38$.
Step 6. $T- = (-3) + (-3) = -6$.
Step 7. $N = 9$.
Step 8. $T-$ is the smaller value and $T- = -6$.
Step 9. When $T = 6$ and $N = 9$, $p = 0.025$ for a one-tailed test. The difference is therefore statistically significant.

How do I report the result?

The above result is reported as:

> According to the Wilcoxon matched-pairs signed ranks test, the difference between the scores from the two conditions is statistically significant at the 5% level. For $N = 9$ the critical value for the smaller T is 8 at the 5% level ($p < 0.05$, one-tailed). As the observed value of T (6) is less than the critical value there is a less than 5% probability that the observed difference is due to chance. Since the difference is statistically significant and since the mean of condition 1 is higher than the mean of condition 2, the null hypothesis is rejected and the experimental hypothesis is accepted.

Suppose the smaller T score was a bit larger, say 10, then we would report the result as:

> According to the Wilcoxon matched-pairs signed ranks test, the difference between the scores from the two conditions is not statistically significant at the 5% level. For $N = 9$ the critical value for the smaller T is 9 at the 5% level ($p > 0.05$, one-tailed). As the observed value of T is larger than the critical value ($T = 10$) there is a greater than 5% probability that the observed difference is due to chance. The null hypothesis is accepted and the experimental hypothesis is rejected.

If you used a computer program to calculate an actual p value for the Wilcoxon matched-pairs signed ranks test then you would report a statistically significant result like this:

> According to the Wilcoxon matched-pairs signed ranks test, the difference between the scores from the two conditions is statistically significant at the 2.5% level [N = 9, T(smaller) = 6, $p < 0.05$, computed $p = 0.0273$, one-tailed]. There is therefore a less than 5% probability that the observed difference is due to chance. Since the difference is statistically significant and since the mean of condition 1 is higher than the mean of condition 2, the null hypothesis is rejected and the experimental hypothesis is accepted.

You may note that we have used the term "computed p" here; see the section "On reporting p values" to find out why.

Test of difference 3: The Mann-Whitney U test

When should I use this test?
This test is used when the data are ordinal or interval, when you are looking to test for differences, when your design is independent measures. There do not have to be equal numbers of participants in the experimental and control groups.

What is the logic behind the test?
All of the scores, regardless of condition, are ranked according to their absolute values – this means assigning 1 to the smallest number, 2 to the next smallest number and so on. These are their ranked values. You then find the sum of the ranked values for condition 1 and do the same for condition 2. If the two conditions differ significantly then there should be a larger rank sum for one condition over the other. If the rank sums are about the same (more or less) then the scores from the two groups do not differ significantly. The actual "more or less" required is calculated in the test.

How do I calculate the Mann-Whitney U test? Example data
- Step 1. Draw a table that allows you to rank the scores from each group (see Table 6.6).
- Step 2. Rank the scores. Identify which is the lowest score and assign a rank of 1, then assign 2 to the next lowest score and so on. Both groups are ranked together and not done separately. For

Participant	Group	Score	Rank
1	Experimental	9	5
2	Experimental	17	13.5
3	Experimental	8	4
4	Experimental	17	13.5
5	Experimental	21	18
6	Experimental	19	16
7	Experimental	14	10
8	Experimental	11	7
9	Experimental	23	19
10	Experimental	25	20
11	Control	6	2
12	Control	12	8
13	Control	16	12
14	Control	10	6
15	Control	20	17
16	Control	15	11
17	Control	7	3
18	Control	18	15
19	Control	13	9
20	Control	5	1

Table 6.6.
Example data for the Mann-Whitney U test.

scores that are the same, assign a value that represents their mean rank (for example, participants 2 and 4 both score 17 and hence share the mean of the ranks 13 and 14, i.e., they are both assigned the rank value of 13.5).

- Step 3. Add the rank values for the experimental group.
- Step 4. Add the rank values for the control group.
- Step 5. If one group has more participants than the other then call it Group B, and the other Group A. If both groups have the same number of participants, then call the group with the smallest rank sum Group A and the other group, Group B.
- Step 6. Find the sum of the ranks for Group A and call it T.
- Step 7. Let Na be the number of participants in Group A, and Nb be the number of participants in Group B.
- Step 8. Enter the values into the formula:

$$U = Na \times Nb + (Na \times (Na + 1))/2 - T$$

- Step 9. Find the value U' by:

$$U' = Na \times Nb - U$$

- Step 10. Identify the smaller of U and U' (regardless of the sign).
- Step 11. Look up the statistics table Appendix 2c. Find the column

corresponding to the Na that you have obtained and the row corresponding to the Nb you have obtained. Identify the value in the cell that meets the identified row and column. This is the critical value. If the smaller of U and U' is less than or equal to the critical value then the result is statistically significant at the 0.05 level.

Worked example

Step 1 to Step 2. See Table 6.6.
Step 3. Sum of the ranks for the experimental group is 126.
Step 4. Sum of the ranks for the control group is 84.
Step 5. The control group is assigned to Group A, and the experimental group is assigned to Group B.
Step 6. T is set to 84.
Step 7. Na = 10, and Nb = 10.
Step 8. $U = 10 \times 10 + (10 \times (10 + 1))/2 - 84. \ U = 71.$
Step 9. $U' = 29.$
Step 10. U' is less than U.
Step 11. Looking at the table Appendix 2c, we find that the critical value is 23. Since the obtained value is 29, then the result is not statistically significant at the 0.05 level for a two-tailed test.

How do I report the result?

The above result is reported as:

> According to the Mann-Whitney U test, the difference between the scores from the two conditions is not statistically significant at the 5% level. For Na = 10 and Nb = 10, the smaller of U and U' is 29, and the critical value is 23 at the 5% level ($p > 0.05$, two-tailed). As the observed value of U is greater than the critical value, there is a greater than 5% probability that the observed difference is due to chance. Since the difference is not statistically significant, the null hypothesis is accepted and the experimental hypothesis is rejected.

If you used a computer program to calculate an actual p value for the Mann-Whitney U test then you would report the result like this:

> According to the Mann-Whitney U test, the difference

between the scores from the two conditions is not statistically significant at the 2.5% level [Na = 10, Nb = 10, U(smaller) = 29, $p > 0.05$, computed $p = 0.112$, two-tailed]. There is therefore a greater than 5% probability that the observed difference is due to chance. Since the difference is not statistically significant, the null hypothesis is accepted and the experimental hypothesis is rejected.

You may note that we have used the term "computed p" here; see the section "On reporting p values" to find out why.

Test of difference 4: The t-tests

Providing your data are at least interval, there is an alternative to using either the Wilcoxon matched-pairs signed ranks test or the Mann-Whitney U test, known as the t-test, although you may not be expected to use it (consult your teacher or tutor). There are several advantages of using the t-test over the previous tests, such as (1) it is a more powerful test, and (2) if you have Excel you can calculate actual p values rather than looking up obtained values against critical values in a table. Note that you cannot do this for the previous tests, unless you purchase (or download a free-trial version) an Excel add-in from the internet.

The disadvantage of using the t-test is that the logic on which it is based is rather more complicated and you may need to know something about statistics that is not on your course syllabus, i.e., the issue of "parametric" assumptions. In fact, there are two types of t-tests, one for repeated measures and one for independent measures.

Parametric assumptions: A quick overview

The sign test, the Wilcoxon matched-pairs signed ranks test, and the Mann-Whitney U test are all known as non-parametric tests. This is because they do not satisfy parametric assumptions. These are:

1. The data on which the test is applied should be at least interval.
2. The data must be drawn from a population that has a "normal distribution".

A normal distribution is a distribution that has a number of features. If you were to plot a frequency distribution of a population of scores and the shape of the curve was "bell shaped" (it has a peak in the middle and it falls off gradually at either end) then it is likely that the distribution is normal. It is often assumed that many measures of human behaviour (and other human attributes) are normally distributed. For example, if you were to plot a frequency distribution of the heights of everyone in the UK, then it is likely that most heights would centre around the mean, and fewer numbers of people would be very short or very tall. In other words, the graph you would plot is likely to be bell shaped. Other examples include weight (presumably), intelligence (but there is a whole debate about whether this is really the case), specific attitudes measured on an attitude scale, and so on.

There are some psychologists who claim that there is no human attribute that is normally distributed. There are two reasons why this argument should be ignored: (1) since it's impossible to measure everyone anyway, we will never know the truth of this statement, and (2) tests such as the *t*-test are said to be "robust" in that they can still be used even if the distribution is not exactly normal (it is said that they are "tolerant to violations of parametric assumptions").

The reason why the normal distribution is important is that statisticians have worked out a good number of statistical properties of this curve. These properties are exploited by tests such as the *t*-test, especially in the calculation of the probability that the null hypothesis is true.

The question arises: How do we know if our sample data are taken from a normally distributed population? One answer is to plot a histogram of the scores of all of the participants in one group, and a histogram for the participants in the other group. By examining the shape of the histograms, one can infer whether the data are or are not normally distributed (see Graphs 6.1 to 6.5 for examples).

Although the data in Graph 6.5 are not as ideally shaped as those in Graph 6.1, we must remember that the assumption is that the

Graph 6.1. An example of normally distributed data. Note that (1) the curve (formed by the data points) is bell shaped, (2) scores are clustered around the centre, (3) the curve is symmetrical about the centre.

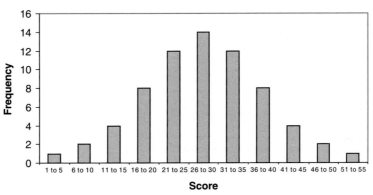

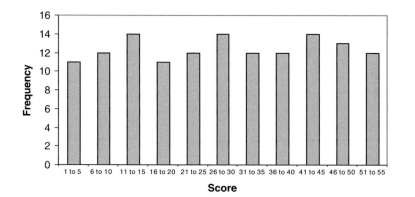

Graph 6.2. An example of a "flat" distribution. The data are clearly not normally distributed.

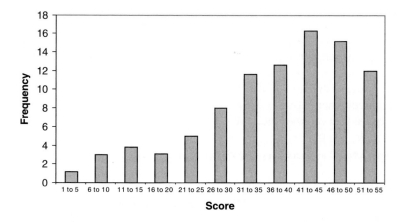

Graph 6.3. An example of a "negatively skewed" distribution. The data are clearly not normally distributed.

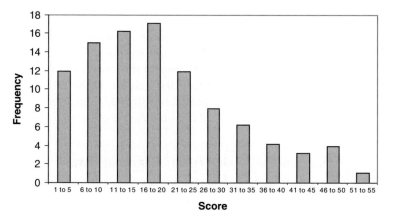

Graph 6.4. An example of a "positively skewed" distribution. The data are clearly not normally distributed.

Graph 6.5. An
example of data
that could be
accepted as
normally
distributed.

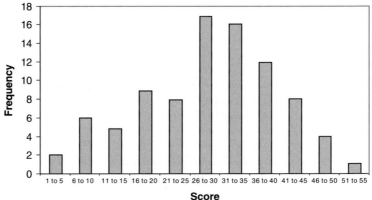

population of scores should be normally distributed, and that whenever we take just a small sample of a normally distributed population it is unlikely that the ideal shape will be present with so few. The more participants we test, the closer to the shape of the curve our histogram will become if our population is normally distributed.

The rule of thumb is: if the distribution of your sample is clearly not bell shaped then assume the population is not normally distributed, otherwise you can assume that it is.

Repeated measures *t*-test (aka Related *t*-test)

When should I use this test?

This test is used when the data are at least interval, when you are looking to test for differences, when your design is repeated measures. The sample of data should approximate to a normal distribution.

What is the logic behind the test?

A measure of the differences in scores between all of our participants (error variance) is used to calculate how much the means should differ by chance alone. You calculate the means and the variances of difference scores between conditions to find the value *t*. If the difference between the two means is statistically significant, then *t* is large, otherwise it is small. The actual size of *t* obtained is compared to that expected by chance.

How do I calculate the related *t*-test? Example data

- Step 1. Create a table of the data suitable for calculating differences (see Table 6.7).

Participant	1	2	3	4	5	6	7	8	9
Scores on condition 1	18	14	17	15	18	19	23	15	16
Scores on condition 2	15	13	14	16	14	11	16	16	16
Difference score	+3	+1	+3	−1	+4	+8	+7	−1	0
Difference squared	9	1	9	1	16	64	49	1	0

Table 6.7.
Example data for the related *t*-test.

- Step 2. For each pair of scores, find the numeric difference (include the sign) and then square that difference.
- Step 3. Calculate the mean of the values in the row labelled "Difference squared", call it M.
- Step 4. Calculate the standard deviation of the row labelled "Difference squared", call it SD.
- Step 5. Let N be the number of pairs.
- Step 6. Calculate *t* by the formula:
$$t = M/(SD/\sqrt{(N-1)})$$
- Step 7. Find the "degrees of freedom" (df) which is equal to N − 1. You do not need to know the statistical meaning of degrees of freedom, but note that in previous tests the critical value was based on the number of participants in the study. With the related *t*-test, the critical value of *t* is based on N − 1, which is known as the degrees of freedom.
- Step 8. Look up the statistics table Appendix 2d. Find the row corresponding to the value N − 1. Beginning with the right-most column, identify whether the *t* you have obtained (ignoring its sign) is greater than or equal to the value in the row. If it is, look at the column heading for the significance level (based on whether you have a one-tailed or two-tailed hypothesis). If no value is found then the difference is not statistically significant.

Worked example

Steps 1 to 2. See Table 6.7.
Step 3. M = 16.67.
Step 4. SD = 23.5.
Step 5. N = 9.
Step 6. $t = 16.67/(23.5/\sqrt{8})$. $t = 2.006$
Step 7. df = N − 1. df = 8.
Step 8. With $t = 2.006$ and df = 8, $p = 0.05$ for a one-tailed test.
The difference is therefore statistically significant.

How do I report the result?

The above result is reported as:

> According to the related t-test, the difference between the scores from the two conditions is statistically significant at the 5% level. For df = 8 the critical value for t is 1.860 at the 5% level ($p < 0.05$, one-tailed). As the observed value of t (2.006) is larger than the critical value there is a less than 5% probability that the observed difference is due to chance. Since the difference is statistically significant and since the mean of condition 1 is higher than the mean of condition 2, the null hypothesis is rejected and the experimental hypothesis is accepted.

Suppose t was computed to be 1.1, then we would report the result as:

> According to the related t-test, the difference between the scores from the two conditions is not statistically signifi-cant at the 5% level. For df = 8 the critical value for t is 1.860 at the 5% level ($p > 0.05$, one-tailed). As the observed value of t (1.1) is less than the critical value there is a greater than 5% probability that the observed difference is due to chance. The null hypothesis is accepted and the experi-mental hypothesis is rejected.

If you used a computer program to calculate an actual p value for the t-test then you would report a statistically significant result like this:

> According to the related t-test, the difference between the scores from the two conditions is statistically significant at the 2.5% level [$t(8) = 2.006$, $p < 0.025$, computed $p = 0.0203$, one-tailed]. There is therefore a less than 5% probability that the observed difference is due to chance. Since the dif-ference is statistically significant and since the mean of condition 1 is higher than the mean of condition 2, the null hypothesis is rejected and the experimental hypothesis is accepted.

You may note that we have used the term "computed p" here; see the section "On reporting p values" to find out why.

Independent measures *t*-test (aka Unrelated *t*-test)

When should I use this test?

This test is used when the data are at least interval, when you are looking to test for differences, when your design is independent measures. The two samples do not need to have the same number of participants in them. The sample of data should approximate to a normal distribution.

What is the logic behind the test?

A measure of the differences in scores between all of our participants (error variance) is used to calculate how much the means should differ by chance alone. You calculate the means and the variances of both conditions to find the value *t*. If the difference between the two means is statistically significant, then *t* is large, otherwise it is small. The actual size of *t* obtained is compared to that expected by chance.

How do I calculate the unrelated *t*-test? Example data

- Step 1. Calculate the mean of the experimental group (see Table 6.8), call it Me.
- Step 2. Calculate the mean of the control group, call it Mc.
- Step 3. Calculate the variance of the experimental group, call it Ve.
- Step 4. Calculate the variance of the control group, call it Vc.
- Step 5. Let Ne be the number of participants in the experimental group and Nc be the number of participants in the control group.
- Step 6. Calculate *t* by the formula:

$$A = Me - Mc$$
$$B = \sqrt{(Ne + Nc - 2) \times Ne \times Nc}$$
$$C = \sqrt{(Ne \times Ve + Nc \times Vc) \times (Ne + Nc)}$$
$$t = \frac{A \times B}{C}$$

- Step 7. Find the "degrees of freedom" (df) which is equal to Ne + Nc − 2. You do not need to know the statistical meaning of degrees of freedom, but note that in previous tests the critical value was based on the number of participants in the study.

Table 6.8.
Example data for the unrelated *t*-test.

Participant	Group	Score
1	Experimental	9
2	Experimental	17
3	Experimental	8
4	Experimental	17
5	Experimental	21
6	Experimental	19
7	Experimental	14
8	Experimental	11
9	Experimental	23
10	Experimental	25
11	Control	6
12	Control	12
13	Control	16
14	Control	10
15	Control	20
16	Control	15
17	Control	7
18	Control	18
19	Control	13
20	Control	5

With the unrelated *t*-test, the critical value of *t* is based on Ne + Nc − 2, which is known as the degrees of freedom.
- Step 8. Locate the critical value of *t* with df for different significance levels (Appendix 2d). For *t* to be statistically significant, it must be greater than or equal to the critical value.

Worked example

Step 1. Me = 16.4.
Step 2. Mc = 12.2.
Step 3. Ve = 34.04.
Step 4. Vc = 26.6
Step 5. Ne = 10, Nc = 10.
Step 6. $t = (16.4 - 12.2) \times \sqrt{\{18 \times 100\}} / \sqrt{\{(340.4 + 266) \times 20\}}$.
$t = 1.618$
Step 7. df = Ne + Nc − 2. df = 18
Step 8. With df = 18 the critical value at alpha = 0.05 is 1.734, one-tailed. The observed *t* = 1.618 which is therefore not statistically significant at the 0.05 level.

How do I report the result?

The above result is reported as:

> According to the unrelated *t*-test, the difference between the scores from the two conditions is not statistically significant at the 5% level. For df = 18 the critical value for *t* is 1.734 at the 5% level ($p > 0.05$, one-tailed). As the observed value of *t* (1.618) is less than the critical value there is a more than 5% probability that the observed difference is due to chance. Since the difference is not statistically significant, the null hypothesis is accepted and the experimental hypothesis is rejected.

Suppose *t* was computed to be 1.785, then we would report the result as:

> According to the unrelated *t*-test, the difference between the scores from the two conditions is statistically significant at the 5% level. For df = 18 the critical value for *t* is 1.734 at the 5% level ($p < 0.05$, one-tailed). As the observed value of *t* (1.785) is greater than the critical value there is a less than 5% probability that the observed difference is due to

chance. Since the difference is statistically significant and since the mean of the experimental group is larger than the mean of the control group, the null hypothesis is rejected and the experimental hypothesis is accepted.

If you used a computer program to calculate an actual p value for the t-test then you would report the first result like this:

According to the unrelated t-test, the difference between the scores from the two conditions is not statistically significant at the 5% level [$t(18) = 1.618, p > 0.05$, computed $p = 0.053$, one-tailed]. There is therefore a greater than 5% probability that the observed difference is due to chance. Since the difference is not statistically significant, the null hypothesis is accepted and the experimental hypothesis is rejected. However, given that the computed p is only marginally larger than alpha, this is a close to significant result and may warrant further investigation.

You may note that we have used the term "computed p" here; see the section "On reporting p values" to find out why.

Test of association 1: Spearman's rho

When should I use this test?
This test is used when the data are at least ordinal (such as data from a questionnaire) and when you are looking to test for a relationship. Note that we use the term alternative hypothesis, rather than experimental hypothesis, when looking for an association between variables because, strictly speaking, studies designed to test for associations are not experiments.

What is the logic behind the test?
The participants are ranked low to high for both measures. The difference between their ranks is then calculated. If the two variables are perfectly correlated then a participant with the lowest rank on one variable will also get the lowest rank on the other variable; similarly, a participant with the highest rank on one variable should get the highest rank on the other. Therefore, in a perfect correlation, the sum of the rank differences will be zero. The degree to which the sum of the ranks differs from zero is what the statistical significance of the test measures.

How do I calculate Spearman's rho? Example data

- Step 1. Create a table of the data so that difference scores for each participant can be worked out easily (see Table 6.9).
- Step 2. Rank the scores on Variable 1, by assigning 1 to the lowest score, and 2 to the next lowest score and so on. For items that are tied, each should share the rank values. For example, in Table 6.9, Variable 1 has a tie for participants 1 and 5, and therefore should share ranks 9 and 10 by assigning 9.5 to each.
- Step 3. Rank the scores for Variable 2.
- Step 4. Calculate the difference between the ranks of Variable 1 and the ranks of Variable 2. You can ignore the sign since it will always become positive in the next step.
- Step 5. Multiply each difference score with itself (square it).
- Step 6. Add up all of the values in the column labelled $D \times D$ (the sum of the squared differences), and call it S.
- Step 7. Find rho by the formula:
$$rho = 1 - 6 \times S/(N(N^2 - 1))$$
- Step 8. Compare your obtained rho with the critical value of rho for N pairs in table Appendix 2e. If the obtained value is greater than or equal to the critical value then the correlation is statistically significant at that level.

Worked example

Step 1 to 5. See Table 6.9.
Step 6. $S = 38.5$
Step 7. $rho = 1 - 6 \times 38.5/(10(100 - 1))$
$rho = 0.767$
Step 8. The critical value of rho for 10 pairs is 0.65 at the 0.025 level. Since the obtained value is greater than the

Participant	Scores on Variable 1	Scores on Variable 2	Rank of scores on Variable 1	Ranks of scores on Variable 2	D	$D \times D$
1	8	99	9.5	7	2.5	6.25
2	5	112	6	8	2	4
3	6	115	7	9	2	4
4	3	88	3	6	3	9
5	8	116	9.5	10	0.5	0.25
6	7	87	8	5	3	9
7	4	78	5	3	2	4
8	3	85	3	4	1	1
9	2	72	1	1	0	0
10	3	74	3	2	1	1

Table 6.9.
Example data for a Spearman's rho test of correlation.

critical value, the correlation is statistically significant at the 2.5% level.

How do I report the result?

The above result is reported as:

> According to Spearman's rho, the correlation between Variable 1 and Variable 2 is statistically significant at the 2.5% level. For N = 10 the critical value for rho is 0.65 at the 2.5% level ($p < 0.025$, one-tailed). As the observed value of rho (0.767) is greater than the critical value there is a less than 2.5% probability that the observed correlation is due to chance. Since the correlation is statistically significant, and since the correlation is positive, the null hypothesis is rejected and the alternative hypothesis is accepted.

Suppose rho was computed to be 0.382, then we would report the result as:

> According to Spearman's rho, the correlation between Variable 1 and Variable 2 is not statistically significant at the 5% level. For N = 10 the critical value for rho is 0.564 at the 5% level ($p > 0.05$, one-tailed). As the observed value of rho (0.382) is less than the critical value there is a greater than 5% probability that the observed correlation is due to chance. Since the correlation is not statistically significant, the null hypothesis is accepted and the alternative hypothesis is rejected.

If you used a computer program to calculate an actual p value for Spearman's rho then you would report a statistically significant result like this:

> According to Spearman's rho, the correlation between Variable 1 and Variable 2 is statistically significant at the 2.5% level [rho(10) = 0.767, $p < 0.025$, computed $p = 0.015$, one-tailed]. There is therefore a less than 2.5% probability that the observed correlation is due to chance. Since the correlation is statistically significant, and since the correlation is positive, the null hypothesis is rejected and the alternative hypothesis is accepted.

You may note that we have used the term "computed p" here; see the section "On reporting p values" to find out why.

Test of association 2: The chi-square test

When should I use this test?

You should use this test when your data are nominal, i.e., when you are looking at proportions of participants who fall into different categories. Typically, the data you have consist of one independent variable (e.g., Condition 1 and Condition 2) and two outcomes of the dependent variable (Option 1 and Option 2), that is the dependent variable can be one of only two possibilities (such as *yes* or *no*).

What is the logic behind the test?

The test compares the spread of scores that would be expected to occur by chance with the actual spread that has been observed. If the observed scores vary sufficiently from scores expected by chance then the result is statistically significant. Whether the scores vary sufficiently from chance is calculated by the test.

How do I calculate chi-square?

- Step 1. For Condition 1, count up the number of participants who responded with Option 1 (and enter it in cell A) and the number of participants who responded with Option 2 (and enter it in cell C, see Table 6.10).
- Step 2. For Condition 2, count up the number of participants who responded with Option 1 (and enter it in cell B) and the number of participants who responded with Option 2 (and enter it in cell D).
- Step 3. Calculate, A + B, C + D, A + C, and B + D.
- Step 4. Calculate A + B + C + D and call it N.
- Step 5. Calculate A × D and call it S.
- Step 6. Calculate B × C and call it T.
- Step 7. Enter the values into the following formula:

$$\chi^2 = (N \times (|S - T| - \tfrac{1}{2} N)^2)/((A + B) \times (C + D) \times (A + C) \times (B + D))$$

Note: $|S - T|$ means "find the numeric difference between S and T and ignore the sign".

- Step 8. Find the "degrees of freedom" (df) which is equal to (number of rows − 1) × (number of columns − 1) = 1. You do not need to know the statistical meaning of degrees of freedom, but note that

Table 6.10.
Example data for the chi-square test.

	Condition 1	Condition 2	
Option 1	A	B	A + B
Option 2	C	D	C + D
	A + C	B + D	

in previous tests the critical value was based on the number of participants in the study. Note that this is known as a 2 × 2 chi-square test (since there are two rows and two columns of data), and the critical value of chi-square is based on df = 1. It is possible to devise a 3 × 2 or a 3 × 3 chi-square test; however, the results become increasingly difficult to interpret, the larger the number of rows and columns.

• Step 9. Look up the value of χ^2 (the notation for "chi-square") in the table Appendix 2f (with df = 1). If the value obtained is greater than or equal to the critical value in the table, then the difference between the proportions in the table is significant.

Worked example

Steps 1 and 2. Suppose A = 19, B = 13, C = 7, D = 13.
Step 3. A + B = 32, C + D = 20, A + C = 26, B + D = 26.
Step 4. N = 52.
Step 5. S = 247.
Step 6. T = 91.
Step 7. $\chi^2 = (52 \times (156 - 26)^2)/(32 \times 20 \times 26 \times 26)$
$\chi^2 = 2.03$
Step 8. df = 1.
Step 9. Since the obtained value (2.03) is less than the critical value (3.84) at the 5% level, the result is not statistically significant.

How do I report the result?

The above result is reported as:

According to the chi-square test, the difference between the proportions of scores is not statistically significant at the 5% level. For df = 1 the critical value for chi-square is 3.84 at the 5% level ($p < 0.05$, one-tailed). As the observed value of chi-square (2.03) is less than the critical value, there is a greater than 5% probability that the observed data is due to chance. Since the difference is not statistically significant, the null hypothesis is accepted and the alternative hypothesis is rejected.

Suppose chi-square was computed to be 4.82, then we would report the result as:

According to the chi-square test, the difference between the proportions of scores is statistically significant at the 5% level. For df = 1 the critical value of chi-square is 3.84 at the 5% level ($p < 0.05$, one-tailed). As the observed value of chi-square (4.82) is greater than the critical value, there is a less than 5% probability that the observed data is due to chance. Since the difference is statistically significant, the null hypothesis is rejected and the alternative hypothesis is accepted.

If you used a computer program to calculate an actual p value for chi-square then you would report a statistically significant result like this:

According to the chi-square test, the difference between the proportions of scores is statistically significant at the 5% level [$\chi^2(1) = 4.82$, $p < 0.05$, computed $p = 0.035$, one-tailed]. There is therefore a less than 5% probability that the observed data is due to chance. Since the difference is statistically significant, the null hypothesis is rejected and the alternative hypothesis is accepted.

You may note that we have used the term "computed p" here; see the next section "On reporting p values" to find out why.

On reporting p values

Note that actual p values are reported in this chapter. According to a recent report in the *British Journal of Educational Psychology* (Wright, 2003), one should always report the actual p value if it is known, since it conveys more information to the reader. In addition, the term "significant" should not appear without being preceded by "statistically", to make it clear that the term refers to the fact that the result is a statistical one and does not imply that the findings of the investigation have psychological significance. The American Psychological Association also recommends reporting actual computed probabilities if they are known. Although it is becoming increasingly popular to report actual computed p values, the approach is relatively new. If you are in doubt, consult with your teacher. A safe way out is to report the actual p value and say why you have done this by quoting from Wright (2003), or say that this is the method recommended by the American Psychological Association.

Notice that in the worked example for the unrelated *t*-test, the computed significance, using Excel, is 0.053. This is only marginally greater than the normal alpha of 0.05. It means that the result is "close to statistical significance" or that the result is "just outside statistical significance". Although you still need to accept the null hypothesis, (a) it is worth mentioning this fact in the results, and (b) you might suggest that there may be an experimental effect if you modified the design a little or tested more participants.

Type I and type II errors

Part of the reason for the trend to report actual computed p values is a concern over what are called type I and type II errors. The purpose of using an inferential test is to make a decision about whether to accept or reject the null hypothesis. There is no half measure – you cannot partly accept and partly reject it. The decision, though, is not really ours to make, since it is based on the test we use and the statistics it produces. This decision can either be the correct one, or it can be incorrect, as Table 6.11 illustrates.

A *type I error* is the mistake experimenters can make when they accept the experimental hypothesis but in reality the experimental hypothesis is false. This can be caused by many factors, such as failing to counterbalance properly, the use of groups that are unequal in important ways, or through experimenter bias. To reduce the chances of a type 1 error (a false hit), you could simply lower the alpha level, say to 0.01. This would make it harder to obtain a statistically significant result. However, in doing so we increase the chances that the other type of error will occur.

A *type II error*, is the mistake experimenters can make when they reject the experimental hypothesis but in reality the experimental hypothesis is true. In other words, the experimenter appears to be too cautious. This can be caused by factors such as errors in recording the data, the unreliability of the method of measurement, too few participants, or poor experimental control. The usual method of reducing the

		The experimenter's decision	
		Accept the experimental hypothesis	Reject the experimental hypothesis
"Reality"	Experimental hypothesis is TRUE	Correct decision (A HIT)	**Type II error** (A MISS)
	Experimental hypothesis is FALSE	**Type I error** (A FALSE HIT)	Correct decision (Correct rejection)

Table 6.11. Classification of type I and type II errors.

chances of a type II error is to recruit a sufficient number of participants. Alternatively, you could raise the alpha level to 0.1 as this
would make it easier to obtain a statistically significant result. However, this increases the likelihood of a type I error.

Generally, most experimental psychologists feel that the value of
alpha at 0.05 gets the balance between these two types of errors about
right. In studies where a p value has been calculated, often it is either
clearly below or well above 0.05, and in these cases the decision to
accept or reject the experimental hypothesis is uncontroversial. It is
when the computed p value is close to 0.05, such as 0.048, 0.06, and so
on, that the decision becomes less convincing. There is no right or
wrong answer in such cases and the overriding rule is that a theory
should *not* be made or broken by a single study – rather a theory
should be assessed on a good number and a good range of different
types of studies.

Two common mistakes in reporting results

Using descriptives to infer differences when the result is not statistically significant

Here's an example of the mistake. The student predicts that the mean
of Condition 1 will be significantly larger than the mean of Condition
2. In the results he reports that the mean of Condition 1 is 56.8 and the
mean of Condition 2 is 50.1. There is a difference of 6.7 and it looks
large enough to infer a significant difference between the two conditions. However, when the Wilcoxon matched-pairs signed ranks test is
used, the probability that this result has occurred by chance is greater
than 5%. In other words, this difference is *not* statistically significant
and $p > 0.05$. This fact is reported in the results. All seems to be going
well, and the student appears to understand the use of inferential
statistics, until we read the words ". . . but since the mean of Condition
1 is larger than the mean of Condition 2, we can reject the null hypothesis and accept the experimental hypothesis." What happened in the
student's brain in the short time gap between the end of the sentence
containing "$p > 0.05$" and the start of the ". . . but since" part? Something has completely obliterated his memory trace of the fact that the
result is not statistically significant!

For an examiner, this mistake is clear evidence that the student
does not understand the logic of inferential statistics. The student is
basing his decision on whether to accept or reject the experimental
hypothesis on the descriptive statistics obtained, rather than on the
results of the inferential test.

A general rule in interpreting the results is this: *If the inferential test reveals that any difference between two means is not statistically significant, then you should treat those means as though they were the same value and in no circumstances should you infer a difference between them.* The test of whether they are different is your Wilcoxon, or Mann-Whitney test, and not a visual inspection of the means.

A similar rule applies to correlation – a positive correlation that is not statistically significant may as well be close to zero.

Of course, the *only* circumstance that allows one to discuss differences between two means (or the direction of a correlation) when the result is not statistically significant is when the computed p value is marginally above 0.05, such as 0.06 (see the section "On reporting p values" in this chapter).

Statistical significance without a tail

Here's an example of this mistake. The student makes a one-tailed prediction that the experimental group will produce a higher mean than will the control group. The means of both groups are reported in the results but not commented upon. The inferential test reveals that the difference between the two means is statistically significant at the $p < 0.01$ level. This is then reported as a highly significant result, the null hypothesis is rejected and the experimental hypothesis is accepted. So what was wrong with that?

The minor detail the student omitted was the fact that the mean of the experimental group, which was 11.75, was *lower* than the mean of the control group, which was 15.5. Although this difference is statistically significant, it is the *opposite* of what was predicted, and so cannot be used to reject the null hypothesis and support the experimental hypothesis.

A general rule is: *The one-tailed experimental hypothesis is not just a prediction about the significance level of the result; it is also a prediction about its direction.* Therefore, both must be supported before you can reject the null hypothesis.

The same applies to correlational studies. A one-tailed prediction of a statistically significant positive correlation is essentially two predictions: (1) it will be positive rather than negative and (2) it will be strong enough to be unlikely to have been caused by chance.

Writing your report 7

What is this chapter about?

There are accepted conventions of how psychology reports should be written. Your report should adhere to these conventions, and they are outlined here. If you follow these guidelines then you can be confident that you have put appropriate information in the right section, and that each section of your report does what it is supposed to do. This chapter also gives guidance on proper referencing, ways of communicating information, and how to adhere to the word limit. Having read a number of examiner's reports quite recently, it is clear that students are losing marks unnecessarily because they are not adhering to these conventions. Make sure that you also read the sections of Chapter 5 about how to present statistical information, as examiners have also mentioned that this is a common area of weakness in student work. When reading this chapter don't forget to read the guidance relating to the specification you are following, as the format varies slightly from specification to specification (see Appendix 1).

Writing your report in the standard format

Psychology reports are written in a standardised, conventional style or format. Unless otherwise stated, it is usual to use the format recommended by the American Psychological Association (APA). Indeed, the British Psychological Society recommends the use of the APA format. The following guide is based on the APA format and offers advice about how to break up the report into sections, what to include in each section, and how to reference other work. It also includes a section on how to write with clarity.

Unless you are required to produce specific headings, use the following main sections for your report: Title, Abstract, Introduction, Method, Results, Discussion, References, and Appendices.

Title

The title should give a reasonable indication of what the study is about. For an experiment, one type is of the form *The effect of [the independent variable] on [the dependent variable]*. This is appropriate when the independent variable involves a difference in the task given to the experimental and control groups (or conditions) Some examples are shown in Table 7.1.

When the independent variable involves a characteristic of a person (their score on a questionnaire or similar) or if it is a correlational design, then use the form *[variable 1] and [variable 2]*. Some examples are shown in Table 7.2. Note that the third example does not consist of an independent and dependent variable, but two variables that are measured for a test of correlation. Notice also that the third title could be made clearer by using the format "title plus subtitle". For example, it could be rewritten as: *Diffusion of responsibility: The number of mothers present and the frequency of infant checking*. This makes it easier to comprehend what the study is about – namely, that it is pitched within the theoretical framework of the diffusion of responsibility (people are less likely to respond to an event that needs attending to, the more people that are present), and by deduction you can work out what the hypothesis of the study is.

Table 7.1.
Examples of titles based on what the independent and dependent variables are.

Independent variable	Dependent variable	Title
Rehearsal/no rehearsal	Recall of a list of words	The effects of rehearsal on the recall of a list of words
Spaced or mass practice	Recall of associate pairs	The effects of the type of practice on the recall of associate pairs
Hint or no hint in instructions	Time taken to solve the candle problem	The effects of instructions on the time taken to solve the candle problem

Table 7.2.
Examples of titles that are based on placing "and" between what the variables involved are.

Independent variable	Dependent variable(s)	Title
High and low stress groups as defined by answer to one question	Scores on the Social Readjustment Rating Scale	Self-reported stress levels and the Social Readjustment Scale
Socio-economic status of mothers	Use of "motherese"	The socio-economic status of mothers and their use of "motherese"
None	1. Number of mothers present 2. Frequency of infant checking	The number of mothers present and the frequency of infant checking

Another popular method is to state the findings! For example, in the study in Table 7.2 entitled *Self-reported stress levels and the Social Readjustment Scale*, suppose that positive results were obtained. In this case it could be rewritten as: *Self-reported stress levels predict scores on the Social Readjustment Scale*. This is a popular method in some neuro-psychological journals. The idea seems to be based on the logic: Look, here's my finding, read my report if you're interested! So it might seem a little brash.

Alternatively, your title could ask a question, as in: *Do self-reported stress levels predict scores on the Social Readjustment Scale?* The logic here seems to be: Look, here's my research question, but you have to read my report (or abstract) to find out the answer! Whichever method you choose, remember that if you have included the variables from your title, you haven't gone far wrong.

Abstract

Your report should begin with a clear abstract, which is a concise summary of your investigation. It should consist of one paragraph that includes the crucial elements of the study. As a rule of thumb, aim for one or two sentences on each of the following: the aim of the investigation, the method, the sample, the results, and the conclusion. Although the abstract appears at the beginning of the report, it is usually easier to make this the last section that you write.

Introduction

The most important message in your introduction is what your rationale for the study is, and this should be based on assessing a particular theory or method. You should begin with a review of relevant theories and work aimed at testing that theory. You then develop reasons why the method and design of your study might clarify any remaining uncertainties or controversies.

Before you begin writing your introduction you should already have formulated your research question. You do not want to just cite any study that you think is relevant to your topic of investigation; rather, the rationale for the study should become evident in your introduction. In developing your rationale you need to show good knowledge and understanding of the issues involved in the topic area. You also need to show that you understand a number of relevant theories that have been developed to explain behaviour in this area. It is often said that a good introduction should provide an "informed commentary" on previous work. This means that it should identify the strengths and weaknesses of a number of theories and studies, and it should specify how these studies have informed the issue under investigation.

The background or "literature review" should be based on *carefully selected* studies. This means two things: (1) any study you mention needs to be *directly related* (completely relevant) to your study, and (2) you must not leave out the most relevant or important study (or studies) on the issue. Typically this is reflected in how much you have read on the issue. If you have read quite broadly, then you will be familiar with the most important studies. If you do not do the reading, then you might not be aware of a very important study on the issue.

One way to approach your introduction is as follows:

1. Begin with a statement, quotation, or everyday example of the issue under investigation and say why it is an important topic for psychological enquiry.
2. Begin with an experimental observation or go straight to Step 3.
3. Provide a brief outline of a theory (usually the first theory developed in the area) that was developed to explain the phenomenon.
4. Provide a number of examples of research evidence that supports the theory.
5. Provide at least one study that has produced results that are problematic for the theory.
6. Either say how the theory was modified OR describe a second theory developed to replace the first theory.
7. Provide at least one example of how that theory is supported by research evidence.
8. Continue the cycle: theory description – evidence for the theory – problems for the theory – new theory, until you have arrived at the specific theory you are going to test.
9. Identify a weakness of the theory, such as an inconsistency, lack of detail, lack of supportive evidence OR if you cannot identify a weakness, identify an interesting prediction of the theory.

Step 9 is your rationale for the study. Although you might not follow these steps exactly, they convey the general approach you should take, i.e., your introduction is concerned with a behavioural or psychological phenomenon and you are discussing different explanations or theories and trying to identify which is the best one. You conclude that you need to carry out another study (yours!) to test which is the best theory to date.

Formulation of the aims and hypothesis/hypotheses
Your aims and hypothesis should be stated *clearly*, i.e., they should not

be vague or open to more than one interpretation, and they should usually be presented at the end of the introduction (unless otherwise stated in your specification). For example, "The aim of the investigation is to examine the effects of caffeine on the performance of a vigilance task, and whether it increases or decreases performance".

Your hypothesis is a *testable prediction* (for example, "Participants who have had three cups of coffee within the last 30 minutes will detect the presence of an auditory target significantly faster than will participants who have drunk nothing in the last 30 minutes"). Since it is a prediction, you will use the results you have gathered to confirm or disconfirm it.

You should state an *experimental hypothesis* and a *null hypothesis*. You should also state whether they are *one- or two-tailed predictions*.

If the *experimental hypothesis* predicts that

> Group A will score significantly higher than Group B on task Z.

then the null hypothesis predicts that

> Group A *will not* score significantly higher than Group B on task Z.

Note that the null hypothesis is stated as a *negation* of the experimental hypothesis. It does not necessarily mean the opposite – the opposite in meaning to the experimental hypothesis would be "*Group B* will score significantly higher than *Group A*". So, we could write the above as:

> The experimental hypothesis of this investigation is: "Group A will score significantly higher on task Z than will Group B". This is a one-tailed hypothesis. The null hypothesis is therefore: "Group A will not score significantly higher on task Z than will Group B".

If we decided on a two-tailed hypothesis we would write:

> The experimental hypothesis of this investigation is: "The scores of Group A and Group B on task Z will be significantly different". This is a two-tailed hypothesis. The null hypothesis is therefore: "The scores of Group A and Group B on task Z will not be significantly different".

Method

If there is one guiding principle on how to write your method section, then it is that you should write to enable your reader to do an *exact* replication of your study if they so wished. This means that you must include all relevant details about your participants, the materials you used, and so on. Any missing detail or ambiguity here could lose you more than just a mark or two. The Method section is divided into Design, Participants, Materials, Procedure, and Ethical issues.

Much can be inferred about the logical thought-processes of a student from the way they have designed their study. When faced with a research aim, there are many decisions to be made regarding the precise way the study will be carried out. This does not necessarily mean that you have to dream up a completely new and ingenious method. What it does mean is that you could modify or extend an existing method, i.e., one used by another psychologist. Even more impressive would be to combine aspects of two different experimental designs. This would show good knowledge and good application.

Remember also that unless your own teacher is marking your report, your marker will only have your report to go on in determining how much work and effort you have put into the design. So, for example, if you spent 8 hours looking through newspapers trying to find suitable pictures for your study, then you should try to make this clear in the write-up, albeit in a fairly subtle way. Don't just say, "Four pictures were chosen from a national newspaper." You could say something like "The investigator carefully studied 85 photographs that appeared in four newspapers and chose four that met strict criteria." By implication, this means you spent a lot of time looking for just the right sort of pictures for your study.

There should be evidence in your report that you followed the design to the letter when you carried out your study. In addition, the design chosen should be carefully thought out, especially in terms of controls and the way the variables are measured. For example, if you wish to measure how much someone likes a set of photographs, you should consider very carefully how you obtain their liking or disliking for each – you should use the same rating scale for each photograph and for each participant, and furthermore, the scale must be easy to use and must be used in the same way by each participant. In addition, you may need to think about whether the participant is to rate the actual content of the photograph, the picture quality of the photograph, or the artistic quality of the photograph (a photograph of an angry dog could be rated as disliked because it invokes fear, or it might be rated as liked because the photograph is interesting and well taken). Your design elements should ensure consistency in the way participants behave and should also ensure they are treated in identical ways (barring any crucial manipulations).

Design

In this section, you should state what type of method you are using, such as a laboratory experiment. You should state what the independent and dependent variables are, how they are measured, and whether they are reliable and valid measures. This should include a statement about what the difference between the experimental and control group is (if not already stated) – or the difference between the experimental and control conditions if using repeated measures. You should state whether the design is repeated or independent measures. You could also give an indication of what type of statistical procedure you will use in the results section, for example by stating that you will be using a test of difference. Control over confounding variables should be outlined here.

Participants

State the population to which the study applies and how you chose your sample. Describe the sample in terms of the number recruited, age range, mean age, male/female ratio, and how participants were allocated to conditions. Describe the sample using other statistics if necessary, depending on the nature of the study.

Materials

Often overlooked by students is a description of the materials the participants were exposed to, and especially a rationale for the choice of the materials. OK, so you used a computer, but the pictures, words, sounds, or questions you gave to your participants were chosen by you for specific reasons. These reasons need to be stated. You must provide a comprehensive list of the materials used (but don't be tempted just to bullet-point your list – write out your list in proper sentences). You should provide evidence of the materials used, where possible, such as by creating an appendix in which to show example materials. If you used a questionnaire then give a flavour of the questions in this section but place one or two completed questionnaires in an appendix.

Procedure

The main purpose of the procedure is to enable a reader of your report to replicate your study exactly. That means the reader should be able to repeat your method in exactly the same way that you did things. In order for them to do this, every detail is essential. Here you describe how participants were allocated into groups, you state the instructions given to participants, and you state the nature of the task they followed. If the instructions were not straightforward or were lengthy, then include them in the appendix and don't insert them here; however, do state the general gist of the instructions and whether (and in what way) they were different between conditions or groups. Describe the task in precise detail, stating any measurements (such as the dimensions of any materials shown, the timing of the presentation of materials, and so on) as clearly as possible.

Ethical issues

In this section you write about how you considered what the ethical issues were for your study. Say what these were and what you did to minimise any risks (see Chapter 2).

Results

Try to record as much information as you can when testing your participants. It may be very difficult to remember which item of data corresponds to which participant at some later point. Furthermore, it may be difficult to obtain essential data from your participants once they have been tested. You can help yourself by thinking about how you are going to analyse your results when planning your study.

Present your results, tables, and graphs, using the standard formats in psychology (see Chapter 5). Keep the presentation clear and well organised. Don't assume that because the marker may be an experienced psychologist they will be able to follow a complicated set of results easily. If you confuse your marker, then they are likely to assume that you too were confused when you wrote up your results. While presentation of your data is important, you are not expected to produce work to the same standards as a graphic designer. It often saddens me to see how much effort has gone into making the graphs (and often the entire report) look pretty, such as using a rare font on the computer and plotting a colourful 3D graph that glows in the dark. In some cases a simple hand-drawn graph can convey more information than a computer-generated masterpiece.

Your results should generally follow this pattern: How you gathered the data; descriptive statistics reported textually and referring to any table or graph; descriptive statistics reported in tables; descriptive statistics reported in graphs; comments on the descriptive results obtained; and (if inferential statistics are to be carried out) the results of any statistical test carried out. Finally, end the results section with a statement about whether the null hypothesis is to be accepted or rejected. Don't forget to mention that raw scores can be found in the appendix.

Discussion

The purpose of the discussion section is to provide: an interpretation of the results; an evaluation of the theory under study; an evaluation of the method used in the current study; the implications of the findings of the study; and suggestions for future research.

Interpretation

Begin the discussion section by saying what the results mean in words rather than in numbers. You need to demonstrate that you fully understand the meaning of the data you have collected and the results you have calculated. You should refer directly to your experimental hypothesis and say whether it is supported or not. Answer these questions:

- What do these results actually mean?
- Do these results support the experimental hypothesis?

Evaluation of theory in the light of the results obtained

You should discuss your results in terms of how they measure up to previous findings. Mention which studies or theories your results support, or are consistent with, and which studies or theories your results do not support, or are inconsistent with. It is important to do this in a thorough way. Don't ignore any relevant research which you have mentioned in the introduction. For example, do your findings which suggest a revision of a theory? If so, in what way should the theory be revised? Alternatively, your findings may suggest that one theory should be rejected. It may be that your findings support a particular theory. In which case, say how your results are consistent with the predictions of that theory. Since we in psychology use our results to generalise to a population, you should comment on whether this is possible in your study and what the limitations might be in your case. For example, we might not be able to generalise from the results of a simple reaction time task in recognising words to the production of words, or from the results from a sample of 25-year-olds to children. Answer these questions:

- Are these results consistent with the pattern of results from previous studies?

- Which theory do these results support?
- Which theory do these results refute or create a problem for?
- How might a theory be revised to accommodate these results?
- Can these results be generalised in any way and what are the limitations in doing this?

Evaluation of the current method

Since research is seldom perfect, you need to identify the weaknesses in your method. Even if you have replicated a previous method there are still likely to be problems with it. Play "devil's advocate" and read through your method with an extremely critical eye. Think about how you could improve the design of your study now that you have carried it out. Ask yourself how you could have chosen a slightly different design and if it would have helped you in your aims of testing a particular theory. Also, you may have found a task too easy or too difficult, or that most participants responded in the same way. In this case you could mention how a change to the design could provide you with a broader set of responses. With the limitations of the study in mind, you should identify any relevant caution we should adopt in accepting the results. Finally, identify any strong feature of the method that is worth retaining or developing further. Answer these questions:

- What are the weaker aspects of the method?
- Now that I have carried it out, what would I change if I had to do it again?
- Given the limitations of the design, is there any reason to be cautious about the results?
- What is the strongest aspect of the design?

Implications of the study for psychological theory development

Research has two main purposes: to understand people better by creating explanations for their behaviour (theories), and to apply this understanding to real-world problems. Ask yourself what your research has achieved in terms of understanding people, i.e., human behaviour, and by paying attention to existing explanations (theories). Then also ask yourself if your investigation has any implications for real-world problems. Comment on what your results might mean for everyday life or everyday problems. Try to think of obvious links to everyday life, rather than obscure ones, and be *cautious*, don't be too grand or sweeping (for example, your results might imply that we should be *more careful* in how we display fear to young children, but they are highly unlikely to suggest ways in which we could *dramatically reduce or eliminate* anxiety in children). Answer these questions:

- How has the study helped us explain some aspect of human behaviour?
- Which theory or theoretical approach are the findings most consistent with?
- Are there any implications for real-world problems?

Future research

Imagine that you are a professional research psychologist and are planning further studies based on this one. Ask yourself what your next study might be and how you would carry it out. Look at the limitations and weaknesses you identified in this study. Could you modify your design for your next (hypothetical) study? There may also be new, related research questions that warrant further research. Try to think about related issues that could be investigated. Answer these questions:

- For each weakness or limitation I identified earlier, how could I redesign my next study to improve it?
- What other kinds of studies could I carry out to investigate the issue further?
- What other kinds of related topics or research questions are worth investigating?

Conclusion

A good conclusion acts like a solid full-stop to the report. Be brief but sum up precisely what you have found in your study.

References

In your report you will be expected to cite previous research by other people. There is a standard format for citing such work in your report (APA standard; see the next section). A list of all the research you have cited should appear in the references section at the end of your report (but before the appendices). You will be marked on whether you have used the correct format, and whether all citations in the text appear in the references section. Your marker may also be impressed by the quality and quantity of the studies you have cited. For example, one or two references is less than adequate, while 60 or more is probably overdoing it. Similarly, references to websites are not as important as references to original journal articles. You should also include a bibliography of anything else you have read for this work that is not listed in the references.

APA referencing style
How to refer to another study (with a single author) in the text
Note: You do not include the author's initials or first names.

> Falcher (2005) proposed the e-space model of learning . . .

> The e-space model of learning (Falcher, 2005) . . .

> In 2005, Falcher proposed the e-space model of learning . . .

How to refer to another study (with two authors) in the text
Note: When two authors are cited in brackets, use "&" to join them.

> Felcher and Felcher (2006) proposed the EBGB theory of memory . . .

> The EBGB theory of memory (Felcher & Felcher, 2006) . . .

> In 2006, Felcher and Felcher proposed the EBGB theory of memory . . .

How to refer to another study (with three or more authors) in the text
Note: Always cite all authors when they are first mentioned.

> Filcher, Folcher, and Fulcher (2007) provided evidence in favour of the EBGB theory.

> There is evidence that favours the EBGB theory (Filcher, Folcher, & Fulcher, 2007) . . .

When the authors are subsequently cited, use only the first author plus et al., as in:

> However, the Filcher et al. (2007) study was flawed on several counts . . .

How to quote a source directly (short quote)
> The model, however, "failed to account for aspects of forgetting" (Fylcher, 2008, p. 23).

According to Fylcher (2008), the model "failed to account for aspects of forgetting" (p. 23).

How to cite a long quote

According to Fylcher (2008):

> The model not only failed to account for aspects of forgetting, it also failed to account for aspects of memory, aspects of reasoning, aspects of thinking. In sum, it failed to account for any aspect of cognition at all! (pp. 23–25).

Reference list

All references are listed in alphabetical order of the first author's last name. Take note of the use of italics for some parts. Journal articles are listed as:

> Falcher, A.B. (2005). The e-space model of learning. *British Journal of Psychological Studies, 17*, pp. 1–77.

This is of the form: Author, initials (publication year). Article title. *Journal Title, volume number*, page numbers.

Books are listed as:

> Felcher, C.D. and Felcher, E.F. (2006). *Models of learning and memory*. London: The Really Interesting Book Company.

This is of the form: Author, initials (publication year). *Book title*. Place of publication: Publishing company name.

Chapters in books are listed as:

> Filcher, G.H., Folcher, I.J. and Fulcher, K.L. (2007). *A critical evaluation of EBGB theory*. In J. Smith (ed.) *A collection of essays on EBGB theory*, pp. 34–121. London: Bullshot Publishing.

Here the book is: Smith, J. (2007). *A collection of essays on EBGB theory*. London: Bullshot Publishing. But this book does not require its own separate entry in the list. The reference is of the form: Author, initials (year of publication). *Title of chapter*. "In" editor initial, editor last name "(ed.)" *Book title*, page numbers of the chapter. Place of publication: Publishing company name.

Secondary references are those where you cite the chapter by

Filcher, Folcher, and Fulcher (2007) but have only read it through another paper, such as Fylcher (2008). You would cite it as:

> Filcher, Folcher, and Fulcher (2007) as cited in Fylcher, Z. (2008). A review of learning and memory research. *British Journal of Psychological Reviews, 12*, pp. 13–18.

Internet documents should be listed as:

> Fulcher, E.P. (2003). *Neurons with attitude.* Retrieved 25 December 2003 from University College Worcester, Department of Psychology at http://www.worc.ac.uk/departs/psycho/Staff/EF/Details.html

It is generally sound advice to cite only internet websites from trusted sources, such as university departments or known organisations (e.g., MIND), or agencies (e.g., the BBC).

Appendices

The appendix or appendices should include raw data and statistical calculations, example materials (such as word lists used in the study, examples of completed questionnaires, and so on), full instructions given to participants, anything important not mentioned in the method section. You can number them using the convention Appendix 1, Appendix 2, etc., or Appendix A, Appendix B, and so on. An appendix *should only exist if it has been mentioned* somewhere in the report. For example, use the format "The raw data can be seen in Appendix 3". An important rule to use when including material in an appendix is: do not let information in the appendix "speak for itself" – this means that you must not put vital information only in an appendix without any indication in the main text that it is there.

Communication

Key words here are *clarity*, *accuracy*, and *format*. To write with clarity means to make your intended meaning clear and unambiguous. To write with accuracy means to be correct in your summary or comments about previous research, and to be correct about the details of your own study. In terms of format, your report should adhere to the report-writing conventions used in psychology.

Some exam boards mention the term "literary expression" in their criteria for quality of communication. This essentially refers to the ability to write in an exceptionally interesting and appropriate way. Students (and professional psychologists) vary greatly on this ability and it is something that is learned over a very long period. However, you do not have to be Oscar Wilde in order to write well, and if you are less than completely confident about this there are a number of rules you could use to improve your literary expression.

First, there are certain standards that should be adhered to when writing a research report. Since psychology is largely considered a science, a scientific writing style is appropriate. This means that you write as though you are addressing the scientific community. Generally, it can be inferred that students who write in a scientific way do so because they read more published research than students who do not write in a scientific way. Alternatives to scientific writing that I have seen are "letters to mom", in which the report reads as an informal, casual, and personal account of the study, and what I call "journalese" in which the report reads either as a voice-over to a TV documentary or as an article in a popular magazine. Neither letters-to-mom nor journalese is a scientific way of writing.

Second, remember that the purpose of research is to be able to discriminate between good and bad theories, so academic authors are mostly concerned with providing evidence for or against a theory or evaluating evidence for and against a theory. With this in mind, note that scientific papers are written in a sort of "argumentative" or "courtroom" style, where the evidence for and against a particular theory is weighed up.

You should also bear in mind that you are not expected to perfect this style straight away, since it is something that is acquired with more experience in the subject. Indeed, try to avoid writing in an academic style if you are unfamiliar with it, as this can sound very strange and pompous to an experienced academic. Your underlying principle when communicating should be to keep your sentences clear and simple – make them read as close to your intended meaning as possible. You should *not* write as though your reader is your marker (so make no reference to your marker at all!), nor should you write as though your reader is an academic psychologist who knows more than you on the issue. In other words, write to an intelligent imaginary person, but one who is unfamiliar with the details of the research in this area.

Third, you should ideally write in the third person and the passive voice. This means avoiding references to yourself: "I gave my participants four tasks . . ." or "I analysed my results using . . .". Instead use "Participants were given four tasks . . ." and "The results were analysed . . .". Furthermore, don't refer to the second person (the reader) with phrases like "as you can see from the graph . . .", but instead use "As can be seen from the graph . . .".

Fourth, spelling, punctuation, and grammar are important in communication since it is essential that your intended meaning be understood. If you write your report on a computer some of this can be checked for you automatically. Many students are often daunted by the amount of specialist terminology used in psychology. Nevertheless, any psychological term you use in your report must be written accurately and used appropriately.

Common errors of communication and how to avoid them

Having marked student work for quite some time now, I have identified a number of common errors that students make which are quite easy to avoid. These can be divided into those that are conceptual and those that are linguistic.

A *conceptual* error is a misunderstanding of a method or concept used in psychology or in research generally. Although the student may actually understand the concept well, the way they use the concept *implies* poor understanding. You don't want to give your marker any unnecessary opportunity to downgrade your work, do you? The following is a list of these common errors and how to avoid them.

Contentious claims.　A common mistake is to think that it's quite OK to make a general or specific statement that seems obvious to you, without actually referring to any evidence for the statement. For example, the statement "In terms of how people choose a partner, we all know that opposites attract" is a contentious claim. Although many people believe in this statement, is there any evidence for it? Such a statement can only be phrased in reference to a piece of research, such as "In terms of how people choose a partner, according to research by Chalk and Cheese (2002), they more often than not select someone who is quite different from themselves in many ways. This lends support to the common belief that opposites attract." This sentence is much more acceptable in scientific writing than the first one. The rule is not to make statements that seem intuitively obvious to you without providing some evidence from research (just referencing an item of research is often enough).

Re-conceptualising reality.　Another mistake is to rewrite reality because you don't understand a particular topic or you wish to ignore a topic that is highly relevant to your investigation. For example, consider this statement: "Although the processes involved in perception are quite complex, as you can see they have been simplified for the purpose of this study." There is no point in trying to hide gaps in your knowledge because your marker won't be fooled. Similarly, if you were to do a study on working memory and failed to mention work by Alan Baddeley (the originator of the concept) then you would be sure to lose marks. Make sure that you have a good understanding of a topic in general and know which are the key studies, so that you can cite them.

A theory does not constitute evidence.   A common, though understandable, mistake is to think that because a theory has been proposed by a prominent psychologist, the theory is virtually fact. For example, the statement "The idea that children learn through stages is supported by Piaget's theory of cognitive development" implies that Piaget's theory is proof or evidence for the suggestion that children learn through a series of distinct stages. However, a theory is an explanation that has been proposed to account for behaviour. It is an informed suggestion that is often based on research evidence, but it is not evidence itself. An alternative way of expressing a popular theory is "Piaget's theory of cognitive development, which proposes that children learn through a series of stages, has received a lot of attention and a good deal of support from research."

Anecdotal evidence.   The use of everyday examples is often very helpful to illustrate a point you are trying to make in your text. However, the example cannot be considered as evidence. For example, consider the statement "Each time I go to the cupboard and tinkle a few knives and forks around, my cat jumps off the sofa and runs into the kitchen expecting to be fed. This shows that classical conditioning is a real effect." Of course while this is an excellent *example* of classical conditioning, it does not prove that is the best or only explanation of the cat's behaviour. There may be other theories that could explain its behaviour. So, the use of such an example would be stated better this way: "Any cat owner knows that each time they go to the cupboard and tinkle a few knives and forks around, their cat jumps off the sofa and runs into the kitchen expecting to be fed. This is a good example of behaviour that may have been acquired through classical conditioning." Don't let this put you off using (brief) anecdotes in your work, as everyday examples, when used correctly, can demonstrate good knowledge of a concept and earn you marks (especially if the example is very original).

Long quotations.   Citing directly from an author is often a good thing, especially when you want to retain the original sentiments of the statement. For example, in trying to point out his belief in the import- ance of animal learning, Tolman (1938) wrote: "I believe that every- thing important in psychology ... can be investigated in essence through the continued experimental and theoretical analysis of the determinants of rat behaviour at a choice point in a maze" (p. 34). One reason why this quote is often used is that it implies that an under- standing of complex behaviour ("everything important in psych- ology") can be gained by studying something relatively simple, such as a rat trying to choose between a left turn and a right turn in a maze. Another is that now, more than 60 years later, the sentence seems remarkably naive.

The point being made here is that the quotation conveys more than just its words. It is a mistake to believe that the use of long quotations, or littering your work with dozens of quotations, implies that you have a good understanding of the issues. You should be selective in your use of them, choosing those that convey a particular sentiment or those that express an idea so succinctly that to paraphrase them would be to lose or distort their original meaning. A related point is that you are required to express ideas in your own words (to show a clear understanding), and if you have relied on too many quotations then you are not providing evidence that you understand the issues clearly.

Note that in the quotation from Tolman, there are three points, "...", and this is standard practice to refer to the fact that I have deliberately left out a word or phrase. So, you do not have cite every word or phrase when quoting someone, but note that you should only leave out that which is not directly relevant to the point you are mak- ing (you do not leave out key points, especially if your quote changes the meaning of the original text – something politicians seem fond of doing when quoting their opponents!).

A *linguistic* error is one where the message is lost because it has not been expressed properly and so for the reader interpretation is dif- ficult. These errors can be grouped by the choice of words, by the construction of sentences, and by the use (or absence) of paragraphs.

Technical terms.   All terms that have been introduced or simply made up by psychologists need a definition. That way you let your (naive but intelligent) reader know what the term refers to and you let your marker know that you understand the term. By a definition, I mean any extra text that can demonstrate what the term means – you do not have to go into a lengthy debate about the term. For example, if you used the term "central processor" in the sentence "Difficulties in attending to more than one task are often said to be due to an over-loading of the central processor", you could add "a hypothetical mental structure that deals with ongoing tasks" in brackets as a short definition.

Use of unfamiliar words.   I said earlier that it takes practice to write academically, and a common error is to try to emulate this style by using what are often called "pompous" terms. For example, "According to Neath (1998), the apportionment of short-term and long-term memory is no longer deemed plausible." The choice of the word "apportionment" is the problem here. Although it sounds grand, more familiar words such as "separation" are preferable.

Comparative terms are completed better!   Words that are used to compare more than one thing on some quality require *completion*. Examples of comparative words are "more", "less", "fewer", "longer", "larger", "better" and so on. When something is "better" it is not an intrinsic quality of that thing, it is only better than something else. For example, "Cowan's theory of short-term memory requires fewer assumptions" is an incomplete sentence because we need to know the theory that has more assumptions, to make sense of the word "fewer". It may be the case that "Cowan's theory of short-term memory requires *few* assumptions", but when using the comparative word, you should complete the sentence, as in: "Cowan's theory of short-term memory requires fewer assumptions than the theory of working memory." So the rule is that whenever you use one of these words, you must finish the sentence by saying what the thing is being compared with. On a personal note, I think that advertisers are much to blame for this, because it doesn't take much to find this error in advertisements ("Better products, better service"). They do this because by law they are not allowed to identify who they are comparing themselves with, so an advert like "Come to Bloggs, we are better than Jones" is not possible. (For fun, log onto www.whatsoninmojacar/adverting_guide.html to see some more examples of how advertisers corrupt the English language.)

Spelling.   It should go without saying that you need to present your work with correct spelling. Word-processed documents can be processed by a spell-checking program, but beware of relying on these completely. If you use one of these, remember to select English UK and not English US (which is often the default).

Incomplete sentences.   Linked to the comparative-term type of error is the incomplete sentence. An example might be "So, in considering all of these theories described in this essay" or "Since the evidence suggests that Cowan's theory is more plausible than Broadbent's theory". The reader of the incomplete sentence is left nodding their head, waiting for the punch-line. The first sentence began with the phrase "So, in considering", which implies that an important point is going to be made *within the same sentence*, not in the next one. The same applies in the second sentence, which began with "Since . . .". I suspect that in most cases the incomplete sentence is created when some editing has been done – an originally complete sentence is chopped up accidentally. The rule is to "proof read" your work carefully before submitting it.

Convoluted or over-long sentences.   If a sentence has five or six sub-phrases in it, for example, then the reader's short-term or immediate memory, which is understood to have a capacity limit of around the seven plus or minus two range for digits (but larger for more meaningful information), is stretched to the limit and as a result by the time they have reached the end of the overly long sentence, of which this is an example to accentuate the point I am trying to make, they have forgotten the first few phrases and the message or messages the sentence is supposed to convey. Don't allow your report to read like a legal contract. These tend to use impractically long sentences to ensure that there is no ambiguity or misunderstanding, which is rather ironic. "Estate agent speak" is another example of the sentence that just keeps running on and on: "The owner of this well-appointed, recently fire-damaged, 4 bedroomed, two-storey property, located close to the waterworks, but not so close that you can smell it, and good for schools, shopping, and travel to major cities, being close to the local railway station, which is handy for that early morning call from the 6:15 to Glasgow, is seeking a quick sale and hence the exceptionally excellent value-for-money asking price for this characterful property that requires complete renovation." Keep your sentences short and to the point! Generally, only try to make one or two points in a sentence.

Problems with paragraphs.   There are two types of paragraphs to avoid creating: The one-sentence paragraph and the never-ending paragraph. Paragraphs are used to help develop a specific part of the text. It follows that a one-sentence paragraph or a paragraph that runs over two pages cannot achieve this. Furthermore, paragraphs should be linked, where possible. An example of such linking is the following (from Lieberman, 2000; p. 6):

> ... Milgram was horrified by the behaviour of German soldiers during World War II who participated in the murder of millions of Jews and other groups in concentration camps. Though some of those involved may have been evil, many seemed to be ordinary soldiers obeying orders, no matter how vile those orders were.
>
> To understand the conditions that could have produced such obedience, Milgram designed an experiment that he hoped would allow him to study obedience in the laboratory ...

The new paragraph begins with the clause "To understand the conditions that could have produced *such* obedience". The word "such" emphasises the key word that links the two paragraphs. Re-read the extract without this first clause in the second paragraph and notice how much "drier" and less informative it seems than with the clause included. Such links give the text a pleasing flow and make it easier to read and comprehend the message.

There are other ways of linking paragraphs, such as:

- Using paragraphs as lists. One way of linking paragraphs is to use them to list your points. For example, you may state that there are three objections to a particular theory. You can then say that the first objection is so, and so, and then begin a new paragraphs with "Second, ...". The next paragraph then begins with "Third ...". (You could also use "A second objection is that ..." and "A third objection is that ...").
- Using key words as links. A common way of linking paragraphs, which works almost independently of the content, is to use key link words such as "alternatively", "finally", "conversely", and so on.
- Asking a question. A good way of linking paragraphs is to begin with a question that asks about the points made in the previous paragraph. For example, the previous paragraph may have described an experiment with a surprising result. The next

paragraph could then begin with a question, such as "What explanation did Curious and Curiouser (2001) offer for this result?", and the paragraph continues with one answer to that question. Use this only once or twice and not with every new paragraph in your report, since it can become very tiresome.

Adhering to the word limit

The purpose of having a word limit is so that (a) students have an idea of how much to write, and (b) a suitable limit is placed on the work involved, which corresponds to the amount the Unit contributes to the course. It is important that you do not go over the word limit and equally important that you are not considerably short of it. A good practice is to do your own word count and state this at the end of the document (see example reports in Chapter 8).

If your report contains all of the relevant information and each section is written in the way described in this chapter, then the likely outcome is that your first draft will be over the limit. If it is under the limit, consider that some sections may need more detail or discussion. If your report is over the limit, then there are several ways of reducing its length. The first is to identify any repetition – are you needlessly repeating the hypothesis or details of the method, or are you making the same point twice? The second approach is to ask yourself whether any sentence is not *vital* to the report. If it is not vital then either delete the sentence or make it shorter (but still readable). The third approach is to try to paraphrase what you have written – for example if the introduction is too lengthy, then try to rewrite it with a view to keeping it shorter and simpler. A fourth approach is to make some assumptions that what you are writing strongly implies that you understand the issues. For example, in Chapter 8 an example report is reproduced on grouping effects in short-term memory. In the discussion, the author tries to make a point about the weakness of the method used. The first draft was this:

> In terms of the method, there was an important weakness. The presentation of items was done by the turning of the pages in a notebook, with the items written on separate pages. This is less than adequate. A much more reliable way of presenting the items would be to display them on a computer screen. That way, a computer program would control the presentation times of the items, ensuring that they were the same. In the current method presentation

times are controlled by the experimenter saying "one elephant, two elephants" to herself to approximate two seconds and by trying to turn each page at the same rate. There is certainly no guarantee that the presentation times and the brief pause in the grouped items were always exactly the same. However, the student did not have the skills to write such a computer program.

This paragraph of 144 words was condensed to only 72 words (reduced by half):

In terms of the method, the presentation of items through the turning of pages in a notebook is less than adequate. Ideally, the items should be presented on a computer screen, with a computer program controlling the presentation times of the items. In the current method presentation times are approximate and there is certainly no guarantee that the presentation times and the brief pause in the grouped items were always the same.

Note that there is a lot of *redundancy* in the original draft. The term "less than adequate" already implies that there is a weakness in the method, so the first sentence is redundant. In the second sentence, we are told again how the items were presented. This is unnecessary because the method section describes it in detail. Another repetition of the method appears later on in the paragraph. The two sentences about presenting the items using a computer are condensed into one in the final version. The final sentence can be deleted because no examiner would expect students to write their own computer programs to control the stimuli.

participants did this then the independent variable would be virtually erased. By separating the participants into two groups, the six-digit group are not exposed to the grouping condition and hence are less likely to use grouping (although spontaneous grouping could still happen).

She's now almost there, ready to begin testing except for one important thing. She has to create a response sheet so that scoring will be that much easier. On an A4 page she creates 6 columns and 40 numbered rows. The participants therefore have to write down their responses in specific places. All she has to do now is to photocopy the sheet and create an answer grid (one with all the correct answers on, so that scoring is straightforward). At the top of each sheet she writes "Participant Number:" and "Group:" so that she can keep a track of which participant was allocated to which group. She works out some standardised instructions that have included some text about the participant's rights and a box to be signed:

> Thank you for agreeing to participate in this experiment on memory. You are going to read lists of digits that you should recall afterwards. In each trial six digits will be shown to you and your task is to write down the digits in the answer sheet provided. Do not read the words aloud. Only begin writing the words after you have been shown all six digits. Write them down in the same order in which they are printed. On the answer sheet are six empty boxes for each trial. So if you are shown 5 6 2 3 4 8, you should write them down in that order, one digit per box. If you cannot remember one or more of them, leave the relevant box blank. There are 40 trials in all. You should know that I am testing 20 people in all and will be interested in looking at their overall results – I am not interested in individual scores and this is not a test of your ability but a test of a theory of memory. You have the right to withdraw from this experiment at any time and without needing to give me a reason. If you have any questions please ask me now.

Rather than begin her literature review in depth or start writing her report, the student decides that it is better to get the testing done and the results analysed before doing anything else. After all, once the testing is done, she is then free to work on whatever section of the report she pleases and at any given time.

For her first participant she is going to recruit a friend of hers who is also doing her A levels (and hence will be sympathetic enough to participate), but not psychology. At the toss of a coin (her method of random allocation of participants into groups) her friend is allocated into the Experimental Group (grouped presentation). The first testing goes well, the timing by counting in her head seemed to work fine, and the whole thing took slightly less than 20 minutes. Only two snags emerged; the first being that her friend wanted to ask a question after the third trial, and the second that she realised that every participant was going to be subjected to the same numbers in the same order. To solve the first problem, our student modifies the instructions to include "Try to work through the trials without asking me questions. There will be opportunity at the end to discuss the experiment." To solve the second problem, she decides to extend the list of numbers in the notebooks by an extra 25%. That way she can start at a different place for each participant. Although the order won't be *completely* different, at least there will be some differences. She continues testing and no further problems arise. For the last two participants, no coin toss is required since she's two short for the Control Group, so they go in there!

The next stage is to analyse the data. She works through each answer sheet to give a total correct score for each place in the list (so she can plot a serial position curve, which might look good) and an overall total of the number of items correct. The first few sheets seem to take ages to score, but it gets easier as she continues. Finally, after scoring all of the 20 sheets (and acquiring a mini migraine in the process), she's ready to enter the raw data into Excel. The data are shown in Table 8.1.

She calculates the total for each participant and the totals for each item in the list (for each group). Looking at the totals, it looks as if the experimental group has higher scores than the control group. She checks that she is looking for differences, the data are at least ordinal, and she is using an independent groups design, so the Mann-Whitney U test seems appropriate to use. She follows the procedure, first calculating the mean percentage recall for each participant and then ranking the totals. She adds up the total rank scores for each group. According to the test, T is equal to the smaller of the two rank totals (82). There are 10 in each group, so Na = 10 and Nb = 10. She enters the data into the Mann-Whitney U test formula and finds that $U = 1$ and $U' = 27$. Looking up the critical value in the table she finds that it is 23 at the 0.05 level for a two-tailed test and 27 for a one-tailed test. "Now," she asks herself, "Do I have a one-tailed or a two-tailed hypothesis? If I have a one-tailed hypothesis then this result is

Table 8.1. The
student's data are
entered into Excel.

	Exp Condition (Grouped pres)								
P	1st	2nd	3rd	4th	5th	6th	Total	Mean	Ranks
1	38	34	33	27	32	34	198	83	19
4	28	34	27	30	33	36	188	78	15
5	23	19	27	24	22	29	144	60	6
7	34	36	35	34	29	37	205	85	20
8	32	23	34	30	18	33	170	71	10
11	34	26	35	29	28	39	191	80	17
12	23	18	29	35	21	33	159	66	7
13	34	22	30	29	14	31	160	67	8
16	33	24	36	33	25	34	185	77	14
18	34	27	32	34	20	32	179	75	12
	Total	Total	Total	Total	Total	Total	Total	Total	128
Control Condition (Non-grouped)									
2	36	32	32	25	31	35	191	80	17
3	27	28	36	33	30	37	191	80	17
6	24	14	18	14	12	28	110	46	1
9	33	34	28	30	26	31	182	76	13
10	27	33	35	30	22	27	174	73	11
14	24	26	29	20	12	29	140	58	5
15	34	15	14	25	14	26	128	53	2
17	31	29	20	17	11	28	136	57	4
19	27	22	11	24	16	33	133	55	3
20	38	22	23	25	21	35	164	68	9
	Total	Total	Total	Total	Total	Total	Total	Total	82

statistically significant, otherwise if I have a two-tailed hypothesis then this result is not statistically significant!" Big decisions!

The theory she is testing is that grouped presentation should produce better recall than non-grouped presentation. Since a direction of the difference is predicted, this is a one-tailed hypothesis. Bingo!

Our student has all of the calculations for her inferential test and she now needs to create a table and plot a graph of the scores from the two groups. She has already thought about plotting a serial position curve, so does this in Excel and produces one for each condition. The curves look a lot like those from the textbooks, so she is pleased.

Working backwards, she works out the experimental hypothesis for the study. A one-tailed hypothesis has the form: [the experimental condition] will [score] significantly [higher] than [the control condition]. Replacing some of these general words with specific details gives her the experimental hypothesis. It has taken some time to arrive at, and she correctly figures that it is worth spending time on specifying an accurate and precise hypothesis. Her null hypothesis is now easy to formulate, since all she has to do is insert the word *not* in the appropriate place. There is nothing untoward about writing the hypothesis this way round. She clearly knew what her hypothesis was before carrying out the testing, she just hadn't written it out yet as precisely as she knew it should be.

She next decides to work on writing the Method while it is still clear in her mind. She writes this with the idea in mind that her reader should be able to do an exact replication if they so wished. Next she writes the Results section. Finally, she's ready to write up her Introduction. She has already made notes and she knows what her rationale for the study is, so it shouldn't be too much of a problem. She focuses on trying to describe a couple of theories of short-term memory and also some experiments that support both. This leaves open a rationale for the current study, which is to provide evidence for or against one of the theories.

The student is now ready to write up her Discussion. She begins with a statement of her results in words and then goes on to say that the hypothesis is supported. She doesn't print out the full hypothesis again here because it is already in the introduction and would just be repetition. She then compares the results with predictions from the theory of working memory and states that the results are consistent with this theory. She identifies weaknesses in her design and makes suggestions as to how it could be improved. She works out some potential designs for future studies that could help to examine the theory. She thinks about how the results could be applied to an everyday setting, such as a memory aid for recalling vital information. She finishes with a definitive conclusion.

Having written most of the report, she can now write a succinct abstract and she can choose a title for the investigation. The whole report is done! However, she considers it as only a "first draft" and decides to re-read the report as though she is not its author. She finds one or two paragraphs that are difficult to read and so amends them. She realises that she has left something out of the method, so inserts it. She does a word count and finds that she is slightly over. She looks for sentences that she could either shorten or delete, as long as such deletions do not reduce the amount of information conveyed in the report.

To summarise this student's approach, the order in which she carried out her study was based on the following steps:

1. Think of a topic for the investigation.
2. Read around the topic, trying to think of an angle or some way in which a previous study could be modified.

3. Think about the actual task you will give your participants in terms of the number of groups, the number of trials, the materials, whether the task is too easy or too difficult, and what your hypothesis is.
4. Try out the task on one or two volunteers first to see if there are any "run-time" problems that need correcting before more people are tested.
5. Test all participants.
6. Collect the data and enter into Excel or a sheet with columns.
7. Carry out descriptive statistics.
8. Create any table that would help with the presentation of the data.
9. Create any graphs that would help interpret the data visually.
10. Write out the experimental and null hypotheses as concisely as you can.
11. Write out the method, while it is still clear in your mind.
12. Write the introduction in full.
13. Write the discussion section.
14. Write the abstract.
15. Choose a title.
16. Read through the report as though you were not its author and make amendments as you see fit, but decide on when you should stop doing this, as it could be never-ending!
17. Do a word count: if you are short, then add extra details of an experiment or study you have discussed; if you are over, then identify any points you have made that could either be paraphrased or deleted as long as the report does not suffer in any way. See the section 'Adhering to the word limit' in the previous chapter.

The student's full report is reproduced below.

The consequences of visual presentation of word lists on the grouping effect

Abstract

The aim of the investigation was to test the working memory model, in particular the theory that the phonological loop is speech based. Lists of six digit words were presented visually to 20 students studying A level psychology. For the experimental group, the lists of words were grouped (two groups of three in each list), while for the control group there was no such grouping. As predicted by the theory, the experimental group recalled significantly more words than did the control group, as found by the Mann-Whitney *U* test of differences ($U = 27$, Na = 10, Nb = 10, $p < 0.05$). These results support the view that phonological coding is based on subvocal rehearsal.

Introduction

Short-term memory has been studied by psychologists for over a century. One of the most influential models in short-term memory was that of Atkinson and Shiffrin (1968). The model consists of a short-term store (STS), which is used to temporarily store information, and a long-term store (LTS), which is a more permanent store. Incoming information is said to enter STS before entering LTS. While in STS information can be modified by encoding, rehearsal, or retrieval processes.

The model neatly accounts for the effects of primacy and recency in a serial recall task. In a typical experiment in short-term memory, a list of items (words or numbers) is presented to participants, who then have to recall the items in the same order. What is often found is good recall for the first few items in the list (a primacy effect) and good recall for the last few items in the list (a recency effect), while items in the middle of the list tend to be recalled least. The primacy effect is explained by rehearsal, which is greater for the first few items. The recency effect is explained by interference, where the most recent items push out older items in memory, so the most recent item is the most vivid.

A number of experimental predictions of the model have been confirmed, such as in studies by Postman and Phillips (1965) and Murdoch (1962). However, there are problems with the model, such as accounting for a number of observations. For example, the model cannot explain easily the effects of phonological similarity, whereby lists of items that sound similar are recalled worse than lists of items that sound different (Baddeley, 1966). The model also has problems explaining the "word length effect" whereby lists of short words are easier to recall than lists of long words and that the effect seems to be dependent upon the time it takes to say the words (Baddeley, Thompson, & Buchanan, 1975). These are the sorts of effects that the alternative model of working memory (Baddeley & Hitch, 1974) was designed to explain.

The working memory model consists of the "phonological loop", which is where items are "subvocalised" (said in one's head without saying them) and rehearsed. It also consists of a "visuo-spatial sketch pad", which is a sort of mental notepad where visual information can be stored temporarily. All of the activity in short-term memory is said to be controlled by a "central executive". The most convincing evidence for the phonological loop is the findings that when lists of similar sounding words are presented *visually* they are still recalled worse than items that sound different when they too are presented visually (Baddeley, 1966). There is no reason why this should be so unless it is assumed that items that are presented visually are subvocally rehearsed. The phonological loop explains this effect quite easily.

However, having a list of items that sound different is not the only way in which short-term memory is improved. Another way is by grouping the items. For example, the list 529*376 (where * is a very short pause in the presentation of the items) is more easy to recall than the list 529376, where there is no gap. This is known as the "grouping effect" and it has been studied mainly by Frankish (1985). Perhaps, then, a more stringent test of the phonological loop in working memory would be if grouping effects remained when items were presented visually. The theory predicts that if visually presented items are visually grouped then they will also be grouped subvocally. So, visually grouped items should be easier to recall than visually ungrouped items.

The experimental hypothesis for this study is:

> Participants presented visually with a list of items that are grouped will recall significantly more correctly than participants presented visually with a list of items that are not grouped.

The null hypothesis is therefore:

> Participants presented visually with a list of items that are grouped will not recall significantly more correctly than participants presented visually with a list of items that are not grouped.

This is a one-tailed hypothesis because it predicts which group of participants will recall more items.

Method

Design

To test the hypothesis, a between measures experiment was conducted. The task was to repeat a list of items presented visually by writing them down from memory. For the experimental group, the items were grouped by showing the first items on one page and the second item on another page, there being a brief pause while the page was turned over. For the control group all items were presented on the same page and hence without the pause. The independent variable is whether the items are grouped or not and the dependent variable is the total number of items recalled for each participant.

Participants

20 participants took part in the study, 17 women and 3 men between the ages of 17 and 18. The mean age was 17.3. Participants were all selected opportunistically as they all attended the same course for which this coursework was done. They were randomly allocated into either group on the toss of a coin.

Materials

One notebook consisting of 90 pages was used to present the stimuli for the experimental group. The book had 3 digits per page and these digits were chosen randomly. A second notebook was used for the control group and it consisted of 45 pages, each with 6 digits per page, which were written in exactly the same order as the first notebook. The only difference was that the first book had 3 digits per page and the second book had 6 digits per page (see Appendix 1 for example pages). Participants recorded their answers on an answer sheet. This consisted of 40 rows numbered 1 to 40 consecutively each with 6 empty boxes where participants could write down their answers in (see Appendix 2 for an example answer sheet that was completed by one of the participants).

Procedure

Participants were given the instructions that the task was a memory task and that they would be presented with pages of digits that they would be required to remember. They were told that they should write their answers down on the answer sheet provided, inserting one digit per box for each trial. They were told to write down the items in the exact order as they appear. They were further asked not to ask questions once the experiment started but told that they could ask questions before and after the experiment (for the full set of instructions see Appendix 3). Participants were given a short break half way through the trials.

The items were presented one page at a time for the control group to the silent count of "one elephant, two elephants" to approximate two seconds. Two pages per trial were shown to the experimental group. The first page was shown for the count of "one elephant", the page was turned and then the second page was shown for the same count, this approximated one second per page. Participants wrote down their answers immediately and in the boxes provided for each trial, and they were given as much time as they needed. In practice, most participants nearly always wrote their answers down within a few seconds. The duration of testing was about 15 minutes per participant. The task was piloted on one participant before testing began properly. Only one minor problem was identified in that pilot (the participant wanted to ask questions in the middle of testing) and so the instructions were modified to request that participants did not ask questions during the experiment.

Results

Each answer sheet was scored and the total number of items correctly recalled in their correct position within the list was calculated. For each participant, the correct number of items per position was also added up in order to see if primacy and recency effects were present (see Appendix 4 for the raw data).

The mean total correct recall of the experimental group was found to be 177.9 items, with a standard deviation (SD) of 19.3. This works out to a mean percentage recall for the experimental group of 74.1%. The mean total correct recall of the control condition was found to be 154.9 items, with a SD of 29.0. This works out to a mean percentage recall for the control group of 64.5%. The data are shown visually in Graph 1 and suggest that the experimental group, as predicted, recalled more than did the control group, but the difference is small.

Since the hypothesis predicts a difference rather than an association, the data are at least ordinal, and the design is independent measures, the Mann-Whitney U test was applied to the data to see whether the difference is statistically significant or due to chance. The difference was found to be statistically significant at the $p < 0.05$ level for a one-tailed hypothesis: the obtained $U = 27$ and the critical value of U at the 0.05 level is 27. Since the observed value is equal to the obtained value then the difference is just statistically significant and therefore the null hypothesis can be rejected.

Out of interest, the mean percentage correct recall scores for

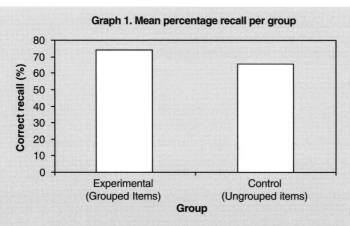

Graph 1. Mean percentage recall per group

Graph 1. Mean percentage recall for the experimental and control groups.

each item in each position was calculated for each group, to see whether or not primacy and recency effects are present in the data and also to see where most of the errors occurred. The data can be seen in Graph 2.

This graph is interesting for several reasons. Firstly, note that for the control group both primacy and recency effects are present. This pattern of data is what should be expected from this type of task. Secondly, note that for the experimental group there are dips at positions 2 and 5. Since the pause occurs between positions 3 and 4 it looks as though there are two "mini" primacy and recency effects either side of the pause. These are consistent with the

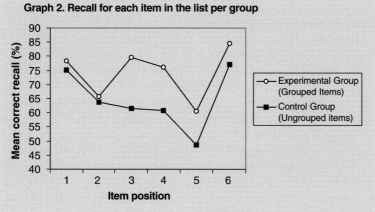

Graph 2. Recall for each item in the list per group

Graph 2. Mean percentage correct recall per position.

findings obtained from studies of the grouping effect. Thirdly, we can see that the effect of grouping is largely to increase the chances that the middle items will be recalled correctly.

Discussion

The results show that when digits are presented visually, if they are grouped then recall will be better than if they are not grouped. While this effect has been found with auditory presentation of digits (Frankish, 1985) the fact that it can be reproduced with visually presented digits means that participants presented with grouped lists are likely to be subvocally rehearsing the items. This is entirely consistent with the hypothesised phonological loop in the model of working memory (Baddeley & Hitch, 1974).

The fact that primacy and recency effects occurred with ungrouped lists is consistent with the pattern of results from many similar tasks and this provides good reliability for the design in the current study. Furthermore, the fact that "mini" primacy and recency effects occur in both halves of the lists with grouped presentation also suggests that the task is reliable, as this pattern has also been found in the literature.

The results support the working memory model and provide data that cannot be easily explained by other models of short-term memory, such as that of Atkinson and Shiffrin (1968). The primacy effect of the second half of the list with grouped presentation can also be readily explained by the phonological loop, since the brief pause allows for better rehearsal of the fourth item. However, the recency effect in the first half is not easily explained. There is no suggested mechanism in the phonological loop that can account for this and hence the theory needs to be modified.

In terms of the method, the presentation of items through the turning of pages in a notebook is less than adequate. Ideally, the items should be presented on a computer screen, with a computer program controlling the presentation times of the items. In the current method presentation times are approximate and there is certainly no guarantee that the presentation times and the brief pause in the grouped items were always the same. Computer presentation would also mean that the order of the lists could be randomised for each participant. However, even with these limitations the fact that such clear results have been obtained suggests either that the effect is a very strong one and/or that the method has not been too weakened by these limitations.

This study helps us understand how information is coded in short-term memory, that is, it is based on a code similar to speech. However, given that the visual information presented can easily be translated into speech, this is not too surprising. Whether such results would occur for other types of information such as music or visual patterns is less than clear. For linguistic information at least, the study has highlighted how short-term memory can be improved. For example, in trying to recall telephone numbers it is suggested that they be learned in groups. There are likely to be many other types of important information in the real world where grouping can enhance recall.

In future studies, it might be interesting to increase the number of items in the lists and to see which is best, grouping by 2, 3, or 4 items. Furthermore, it may be useful to try to inhibit rehearsal to see if the grouping effect is lost with visual presentation. This is certainly the case with visual presentation and the acoustic similarity effect (Baddeley, 1966) and such a result would provide further supportive evidence of working memory. Since little is known about the hypothesised visuo-spatial sketch pad, one way of approaching its study would be to examine visually grouped items that are non-linguistic but visual, to see if this system behaves in a similar way to the phonological loop or even whether this system is involved in the grouping effect observed in this study.

This study has found that grouping effects occur in short-term memory even when the items are presented visually. This implies that the hypothesised phonological loop in working memory operates on an acoustic, speech-based code. The results are therefore consistent with this model and provide further support for it.

Word count: 2,476

References

Atkinson, R.C. & Shiffrin, R.M. (1968) cited in Eysenck, M.W. (2003). *Psychology for AS level*. Hove: Psychology Press.

Baddeley, A.D. (1966) cited in Eysenck, M.W. (2003). *Psychology for AS level*. Hove: Psychology Press.

Baddeley, A.D. & Hitch, G.J. (1974) cited in Eysenck, M.W. (2003). *Psychology for AS level*. Hove: Psychology Press.

Baddeley, A.D., Thompson, N., & Buchanan, M. (1975) cited in Neath, I. (1998). *Human memory: An introduction to research, data, and theory*. Pacific Grove: Brookes/Cole.

Frankish, C. (1985). Modality-specific grouping effects in short-term memory. *Journal of Memory and Language, 24*, 200–209.

Murdock, B.B. (1962) cited in Fulcher, E.P. (2003). *Cognitive psychology*. Exeter: Learning Matters.

Postman, L. & Phillips, L.W. (1965) cited in Fulcher, E.P. (2003). *Cognitive psychology*. Exeter: Learning Matters.

Appendix 1: Examples of pages from the list presented to participants.

Appendix 2: An example answer sheet completed by one of the participants.

Appendix 3: The standardised instructions.

Example report 2: A laboratory experiment

This is an example of an experiment to test the theory that classical conditioning can explain how we come to like or dislike something in certain situations. The study is almost a straight replication of previous research, but the material used is different. This way there is an original angle to the design and this can test the limitations of the underlying theory. I've chosen the particular topic because I feel it might be an interesting slant on an age-old question: Do we judge people by the company they keep? Pay attention to the way the report is written up: how the introduction tries to develop a rationale for the study, the way the counterbalancing method is explained in the procedure, the presentation of the result, and the way the discussion tries to answer all of the questions I listed in Chapter 7 that a discussion should address. In terms of the topic, although this is not based on a real experiment that was actually carried out, it is typical of experiments that are reported under the terms *evaluative conditioning, evaluative learning,* and *classical conditioning of attitudes*. The results, too, are quite typical of what you would find in the literature.

Can the attractiveness of a man be affected by the company he keeps?

Abstract
This investigation attempted to establish whether everyday likes and dislikes can be changed through classical conditioning. In

particular, whether the rating of a man's face changed depending upon whether he had been previously "paired" with an attractive woman or an unattractive woman. The results showed that men paired with unattractive women were rated as less attractive than men paired with attractive women. These results appear to support the view that everyday liking can be changed through classical conditioning.

Introduction

Our feelings towards person names are remarkably strong. This is especially evident when a family chooses the name for a new baby. One reason why we may strongly dislike a name is because it reminds us of someone we strongly disliked in our past. For some reason we are unable to detach the name from the person. One explanation of how we come to dislike something as innocuous as a name is through classical conditioning.

The first experiments in classical conditioning were carried out by Pavlov (1849–1936). When the bell was repeatedly paired with the presentation of food, the dog then learned to salivate to the bell. The bell is referred to as the conditioned stimulus (CS), the food as the unconditioned stimulus (UCS), and the learned response as the conditioned response (CR). In terms of person names, the name may be the CS, the unpleasant person the UCS, and the strong disliking of the name, the CR.

The question is whether classical conditioning is a form of learning that is not just specific to reflexes (such as salivation) but can provide an explanation of how we come to like and dislike things. There is some evidence for this as the study by Levey and Martin (1975) shows. Using a classical conditioning procedure, ordinary picture postcards (previously rated as neutral) that were paired with strongly liked postcards were rated as more liked than other previously neutral postcards that were paired with strongly disliked postcards. The pairings involved merely showing the postcards together. This shows that liking and disliking of everyday objects can occur through classical conditioning. More recent studies have replicated this result many times over (e.g., Baeyens et al., 1990; and De Houwer et al., 1994).

However, in a recent study several experiments were reported where the effect did not occur (Rozin et al., 1998). These experiments included pairing bland patterns with insects, and pairing product names with a pleasant odour. Such failures to find changes in likes and dislikes (towards the patterns or product names) may cast doubt on whether we learn this through classical conditioning.

A further problem is that in most studies, pictures or words are paired in an arbitrary manner. For example, neutral postcards have been paired with liked or disliked postcards, and "neutral words" have been paired with "pleasant words" or unpleasant words. The problem with such demonstrations of classical conditioning is that they may have limited application, since the stimuli are rather innocuous. It may be better to use stimuli that have more of a social significance, such as photographs of people, and to test the prediction that the perception of an individual can be altered by the people he or she is seen with.

The aim of the present study is to use more relevant stimuli to everyday life and to see how far the effect, if it is present, can extend to our liking and disliking of people. This will be done by pairing photographs of men who are deemed neither attractive nor unattractive (termed "neutral"), with photographs of either attractive or unattractive women.

The experimental hypothesis of the study is:

> The ratings of men paired with women rated as highly attractive will be significantly *higher* than the ratings of men paired with women rated as unattractive.

The null hypothesis is therefore:

> The ratings of men paired with women rated as highly attractive will not be significantly *higher* than the ratings of men paired with women rated as unattractive.

This is a one-tailed prediction because we are predicting the direction of the difference.

Method

Design

The independent variable is whether the photograph of a woman, paired with that of a neutral man, was classed as attractive (W+) or unattractive (W−) by a panel of raters. The dependent variable is the actual ratings of the photographs of the men. The study used a repeated measures design with all participants exposed to the two conditions, which were:

Condition 1: Photographs of men paired with W+.
Condition 2: Photographs of men paired with W−.

Participants

24 participants, 18 women and 6 men, each studying A level psychology in an evening class. The age range was 18 to 32, and the mean age was 21.9 years.

Materials

40 photographs of men and 40 photographs of women were downloaded from the internet. The photographs were then resized to 8 × 6 cm (portraits) and printed off in black and white and stuck to card. The faces selected were of non-famous persons and the features of the face were clearly visible. A panel of raters, 22 students studying for their A levels then rated each photograph on a ten-point scale from "1 = very unattractive" to "10 = very attractive". The point 5 was labelled "neither attractive nor unattractive". The mean ratings for the two lots of 40 photographs were then calculated, and the rank order was found for each sex. The middle 18 photographs of men were chosen for the experiment, the top 6 and bottom 6 photographs of women were chosen for the W+ and W− sets, respectively.

Procedure

Counterbalancing was required because we could not always pair the same faces for all participants. Therefore the pairings switched for two counterbalancing groups, such that for some participants the same man was paired with a W+ and for others it would be paired with a W−. To do this the photographs of men were divided into two sets and the participants were divided into two counterbalancing groups. For each group, the set paired with each type of women was swapped (see Table 1).

The photographs of men were randomly allocated into Set 1 or 2. The participant was shown each pair in turn and the order of the pairs was randomised. The experimenter worked through the

Rating of women	Group 1	Group 2
W+	Set 1	Set 2
W−	Set 2	Set 3

Table 1. Rotation used for counterbalancing. For example, the photographs of men in Set 1 were paired with attractive women (W+) for Group 1, and with unattractive women (W−) for Group 2.

cards three times, a total of 54 trials in all. The participant was told that these are couples that have recently got married.

Next, the photographs of the men were presented alone, and the participant had to rate each of them on the same 10-point scale described above.

Ethical procedures

All participants were told that they had the right to withdraw at any time and without giving a reason. To ensure anonymity of the data, no names were recorded and participants were tested individually and in isolation from other people. Although a cover story was used, it was felt that the small amount of deception was necessary so that awareness of the hypothesis would not influence their behaviour. All participants were appropriately debriefed (by running through the aims of the study and expected findings) and thanked at the end of the study.

Results

To confirm that the attractiveness of the women in each condition was sufficiently different, the mean ratings were calculated. The mean rating of the W+ set was 9.2 and the mean rating of the W− set was 3.8 (see Graph 1). As can be seen from Graph 1, the W+ set were indeed rated more attractive than the W− set.

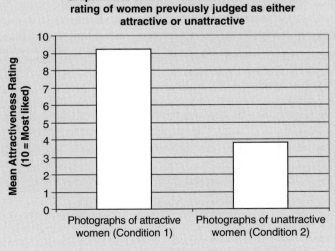

Graph 1. Bar chart of the mean attractiveness rating of women previously judged as either attractive or unattractive

Graph 1. Mean attractiveness ratings of the two sets of photographs.

	Mean Attractiveness Rating	Standard Deviation
Photographs of men paired with photographs of attractive women (Condition 1)	6.3	3.59
Photographs of men paired with photographs of unattractive women (Condition 2)	2.8	2.86

Table 2. Summary statistics for the ratings of men paired with attractive or unattractive women.

Ratings of the photographs of the men

The mean rating of the photographs of the men paired with W+ was 6.3, with a standard deviation of 3.59. The mean rating of the photographs of the men paired with W– was 2.8, with a standard deviation of 2.86. These results are shown in Table 2. The differences between these means can be seen visually in Graph 2.

As can be seen from both Table 2 and Graph 2, the photographs of men paired with W+ are rated as more liked (have a higher mean rating) than the photographs of men paired with W–.

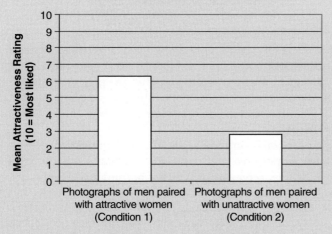

Graph 2. Bar chart of the mean attractiveness rating of men paired with women previously rated as either attractive or unattractive

Graph 2. The mean attractiveness ratings of photographs of men paired with women previously rated as either attractive or unattractive.

To establish whether the difference between the mean ratings between the two conditions is statistically significant, a Wilcoxon matched-pairs signed ranks test was carried out on the data. This test was chosen because it is suitable for (1) testing for differences between conditions (2) the design is repeated measures, and (3) the data are ordinal (at least).

The difference between the scores from Condition 1 and Condition 2 is statistically significant at the 5% level. For $N = 24$ the critical value for the smaller T is 91 at the 5% level ($p < 0.05$, one-tailed). As the observed value of T (73) is less than the critical value there is a less than 5% probability that the observed difference is due to chance. Since the difference is statistically significant and since the mean of Condition 2 is lower than the mean of Condition 1 (as predicted), the null hypothesis is rejected and the experimental hypothesis is accepted. This means that the photographs of the men that were paired with photographs of attractive women were rated as more liked than the photographs of the men paired with the photographs of unattractive women.

Discussion

The results of the study show that pairing a photograph of a man with an unattractive woman can result in the man being rated as less attractive than if he had been shown with a more attractive woman. The result means that the perception of attractiveness of a man can be affected by the attractiveness of a woman he is associated with. Since the result occurs purely by the association of two photographs (no other information being provided) then the effect is likely to have occurred by classical conditioning.

However, the results only show such differences between the two groups of photographs. Because we did not collect attractiveness ratings of the men before and after the pairing trials, we cannot be sure that any changes to the ratings have taken place. It may be, for example, that the first set of photographs of men were more generally liked anyway.

In a practical, everyday sense, the result means that there is a tendency to perceive men who are associated with unattractive women as themselves unattractive – her unattractiveness appears to "rub off" onto the man. Conversely this also appears to work when the men are associated with attractive women – her attractiveness appears to "rub off" onto the man. These results confirm the theory of Baeyens et al. (1990) that liking and disliking can change through classical conditioning.

One weakness of the method was in the way the photographs were paired. We told participants that these were couples who have recently got married. However, the photographs varied in quality and were clearly not taken at the same time. As such, the cover story was less than convincing. This could have had either of two opposing effects: either it may have caused participants to become aware of the purpose of the study and hence they may have conformed to what was expected of them, or it may have even weakened or "diluted" the classical conditioning effect, meaning that the effect is even stronger than the present results indicate. However, given that no participant showed any signs either during or after the experiment that they were aware of the true nature of the study, we are tempted to conclude that the result is a reliable one.

In a future study, we could select photographs from the "wedding announcements" section of a local newspaper. This way, we could be more confident that (1) the photographs were similar in quality and (2) the fact that the models are dressed in wedding "outfits" would give greater credence to the cover story.

A related problem is that by using a panel of raters to determine which women were attractive and which were unattractive, it is assumed that attractiveness is universal, which it may not be. One person's picture of perfection may be another person's "turn-off". So clearly, if this is the case then using a rating panel may have watered down any effects, as a woman placed in the unattractive category may have been perceived as attractive by a good proportion of the participants.

A replication study, with the above changes, might help us to determine whether the effect is truly dependent upon classical conditioning. In terms of everyday life, the findings of the present study suggest that people's likes and dislikes can be affected by association. The results may also be considered as of concern since if something as arbitrary as an association can promote liking or disliking then in certain cases society should be careful about the sorts of associations we create, especially those in the media (such as thinness with glamour, sophistication with smoking, and happiness with alcohol).

Word count: 2,190

References

Baeyens, F., Eelen, P., & Van den Bergh, O. (1990). Contingency awareness in evaluative conditioning: A case for unaware affective-evaluative learning. *Cognition and Emotion, 4*, 3–18.

De Houwer, J., Baeyens, F., & Eelen, P. (1994). Verbal evaluative conditioning with undetected stimuli. *Behaviour Research and Therapy, 32*, 629–633.

Levey, A.B. & Martin, I. (1975). Classical conditioning of human "evaluative" responses. *Behaviour Research and Therapy, 13*, 221–226.

Rozin, P., Wrzesniewski, A., & Byrnes, D. (1998). The elusiveness of evaluative conditioning. *Learning and Motivation, 29*, 397–415.

Appendix A: Examples of the photographs used in the study.

Appendix B: Raw data and statistical calculations.

20 ideas for an investigation 9

What is this chapter about?

Ideas don't come easily and although I have suggested ways of thinking about how to design your own investigation in earlier chapters, there is nothing like seeing a few examples to get you thinking. In this chapter there are 20 suggestions (plus variations on these) for an investigation. I provide an outline of the rationale of the investigation, how to design the study, how to prepare the materials, what kind of hypothesis to use, and how you might approach analysing the data. Read carefully though the topics that interest you and either follow the design suggested or think about how you could modify the design in some way.

1. Primacy and recency in impression formation

You could devise an experiment to test the theory that there is a primacy effect in impression formation, rather similar to the studies by Asch (1946) and Luchins (1957). In those studies participants were given a list of traits or a story about a character where the description of his or her personality changed halfway through. Participants rated the character on a list of adjectives. It appears that the first half of a list or story generally gives a more lasting impression of the character than the second half. Perhaps primacy works because people need to hold onto their first impression and merely interpret new information in terms of the impression they already have. The problem with these studies is that they are rather artificial – why should we really form an impression of a textual description of someone we know does not exist?

One way of improving ecological validity might be to identify the impressions people have of a number of famous people. You could then tell your participants that as a result of reading a number of "gossip" magazines and several tabloid newspapers you have new information about each person – something they have said or done that contrasts to their popular image. Give them that information and see if their impression changes. You could mix plausible and bizarre stories about the person, to see if the more unlikely the story is, the more people's impression changes. Also think of positive stories (e.g., did a hundred-mile walk for charity) as well as negative stories (e.g., beat up a photographer so badly they were put into hospital). To rate them you could use adjectives, such as those Table 9.1.

You can tot up the number of positive descriptors and negative descriptors given to each person before and after reading the stories you create. If you don't like this scoring system because it is too inflexible, you could choose the most important ones and get the participants to rate them on a scale of 1 to 10 (e.g., 1 = most ungenerous, 5 = neither generous nor ungenerous, 10 = most generous). Remember to fully debrief them afterwards – they should know that you have completely made up these stories. With this in mind, don't invent stories that are too alarming (e.g., concerning murder or child abuse). Remember, we have no right to upset our participants.

2. Experiencing prejudice as a way of reducing prejudice

Weiner and Wright (1973) aimed to test the possibility that prejudice can be lessened when participants directly experience what it feels like to be the subject of prejudice. Although there are serious ethical problems with such studies, you could design a version that gets the participant "into the mind" of someone experiencing prejudice, through literature. Identify a passage of text that describes the painful experiences of prejudice (such as the story of Rosa Parks who refused to give up her seat on a bus to a white man, or text from an author

Table 9.1.
Example words for a study in primacy and recency in impression formation.

generous – ungenerous	humorous – humourless	important – insignificant
wise – shrewd	sociable – unsociable	humane – ruthless
happy – unhappy	likeable – unlikeable	good looking – unattractive
charitable – uncharitable	responsible – irresponsible	stable – unstable
serious – jolly	altruistic – self-centred	broad minded – narrow minded
honest – dishonest	good role model – poor role model	strong character – weak character

such as Maya Angelou). Before your participants read the text, and after, administer a form of the Bogardus Social Distance Scale to see if there are any changes in their attitudes. In this scale you invite the participant to place a tick against how they would feel about a person from a minority group (1) being allowed entry into your country in large numbers, (2) living in your city, (3) living in your neighbourhood, (4) living in your street, (5) living next door to you, (6) befriending you, (7) marrying someone of your close family. The point at which a participant does not place a tick is their distance score. So if someone ticks OK up to question 5 then they score 5, since that is the first point at which they show negative feelings. You can apply the set to more than one minority group to get a broader score (by adding up a participant's score against each minority).

For your data you will have scores before and scores after. You are looking for a test of difference, and the design is repeated measures. There are several ways in which ethics should be considered here. The first is that some participants could be a little anxious about answering such questions, and a second is that you might find out something unwelcome about someone you know or are fond of. To avoid these as much as possible, try to use participants whom you do not know or are unlikely to know in the future. A third problem is that you could easily offend someone from a minority group. To avoid this, you might discuss the questionnaire with someone from a minority group for their views, especially on how you should word the questionnaire.

3. Evolutionary theories of interpersonal attraction

According to evolutionary theories, there should be a difference in the way men choose women as partners and the way women choose men as partners in heterosexual relationships. Davis (1990) carried out a study on personal ads in newspapers. Women looking for men tended to look for "success objects" and men looking for women tended to look for "sex objects". This tends to support evolutionary theory that men should seek younger, very fertile women, and women should seek men with protective resources (who are also stable). The theory also predicts that men should advertise themselves as having protective resources and women should emphasise their physical attractiveness or willingness to have sexual relations. So the idea for this study is to analyse the way heterosexual men and women advertise themselves, rather than analysing what they say they are looking for. The study would be a content analysis of "lonely hearts" columns in local newspapers or from the internet. For example, I found something that reads similar to this:

> Man: I'm told that I am good looking. I am 52, single, never been married, have no kids or ties, very passionate, very caring and sensual, very affectionate and kind. Good natured, and a loving personality. Have holiday home in the sun. I am seeking an attractive single female aged between 32–54 for fun and friendship.

For men we would be looking to count any adjective or single phrase that is either (a) consistent with "man with protective resources" or (b) inconsistent with "man with protective resources". In the above, this ad would score 9 for consistency ("single", "no ties" – therefore no one else with whom to share his resources; "passionate", "caring", "affectionate", "kind", "good natured", "loving" = has the emotional capacity to protect; "holiday home" = must be quite affluent to be able to afford one of these) and 1 for inconsistency ("never been married" – and therefore possibly unstable). An alternative way of scoring would be to award only 3 for consistency, because some of the terms mean much the same thing, i.e., an emotional capacity to protect. You would then choose a similar method of scoring for women.

The data you will have will comprise a set of scores on consistency and inconsistency for men, and similar for women. For the men's data you can do a repeated measures test of differences; with the prediction that consistency scores will be higher than inconsistency scores. You then do a similar analysis for women.

4. Observing a diffusion of responsibility

Latané and Darley (1970) used the concept of diffusion of responsibility to explain why bystanders to a crime or incident fail to act. The more people that are present, the greater is the assumption that someone else will respond. A single bystander has a greater sense of responsibility because there is no one else around to help but them. An interesting generalisation of the concept would be to study the responsibility for checking a child in a mother-and-toddler group. Under normal circumstances, a mother will constantly check her child to make sure that he or she is not in danger (such as about to grab something sharp or about to put some rubbish into his or her mouth, and so on). The theory of the diffusion of responsibility would predict in this setting that the more mothers that are present, the less each mother will check her child. It predicts this because the mother knows that other people are present who are equally aware of dangers and who are perhaps equally likely to keep an eye on her child. For this investigation, you would have to obtain permissions to observe mother–child interactions. You would look at different groups of mothers, noting how many mothers are in the group and how many children they are collectively looking after. Looking at one group at a time, record every occasion that a mother checks a child in a non-verbal way (such as turning her head to a child), in a verbal way (such as "Put that down sweetie!"), or in a behavioural way (such as going up to the child and taking something from it or picking it up, and so on). The interesting question is how these checking scores vary as the number of mothers in the group increases. The prediction is that they will be lower for larger groups. Hence this would be a correlation for each measure you test (non-verbal, verbal, and behavioural checks) with the number of mothers in the group. You would look at, say, 10 different groups of mothers (where a group is defined by two or more mothers in close proximity and talking together), and give yourself a time limit (the same amount of time per group) for recording your observations, say 10 to 15 minutes with each group.

5. Learning as a function of sleep

There are several theories of why we need sleep or what happens to us physiologically and psychologically when we are asleep. One theory is that sleep, or rather dreaming, serves the role of improving memory (e.g., Crick & Mitchison, 1983; Webb & Cartwright, 1978). To test the theory that sleep improves memory, you could conduct an investigation on the learning of some task (e.g., a list of words, a maze, or some other type of puzzle). You would need two groups of participants. One would be the no-sleep group, who are given the opportunity to learn the information at 9 in the morning and then tested at 9 in the evening. A second group, the sleep group, are given the information at 9 in the evening and are then tested at 9 the following morning. Both groups are tested 12 hours apart, except that one group has had a period of sleep in between learning and testing, but the other group has not.

Although there may be many other confounding variables in the study (and you could gain marks by identifying these), at least the theory predicts that the sleep group would show better learning than the no-sleep group, and if that doesn't happen then you have problematic evidence for the theory. This investigation would have two independent groups and you would be looking at the differences in the scores from the two groups on the task.

To put an extra slant on the study, since many theories relate to the act of dreaming rather than just sleep, you could ask participants to record whether they woke up that morning in the middle of a dream. So, for the sleep group you could divide them into those who were dreaming when they awoke (the dream group), and those who were not dreaming when they awoke (the no-dream group). Since dreaming is supposed to enhance memory, those who woke in the middle of a dream should show *less* learning than those who did not wake in a dream. The reason for this is that dream group have had their dream interrupted and hence the process that supports learning has been terminated before it has been completed. You could do an independent groups comparison of the dream versus no-dream groups.

6. Spaced versus massed practice

Several studies show that people learn more when they take a short break between each learning session (spaced practice) than when they do not take breaks (massed practice). Examples from the literature include Lorge (1930) who examined the effects of practice on a mirror-drawing task (drawing around a star shape by looking in a mirror). Interestingly, learning after 20 trials with massed practice (no break) was the same as learning after only 5 trials with spaced practice (one day between trials). Other studies include Underwood (1961) and Keppel (1967), who have noted the huge amount of memory loss that goes with massed practice. Such remarkable results say a lot about student studying habits – they prescribe a pattern of study whereby you spend about 30 minutes a day merely reading through your material and course books, rather than doing this on selected days. For example, the research suggests that up to four-fifths of the time spent in one very long revision session could be completely wasted (that's four out of every five hours), when compared to five days of revision with just one hour in each.

You could design a study for your investigation that compares massed practice with spaced practice. Your rationale is that most previous studies have looked at free recall, where the participant is not given cues during testing. You could investigate whether there are similar effects on recognition. This is a much more demanding hypothesis to satisfy, since recognition is superior to recall. Nevertheless, given enough trials an effect might emerge. You simply present to your participants lists of paired associates, word pairs that have no previous relationship such as table–control, force–ordinal, below–groom, and so on. Then during recognition you present each cue and the participant has to recognise the correctly associated word. So you present 'table' and they have to choose between 'groom', 'king', 'control' (one is correct, one is from another pair, and one is new). The two groups of participants are a massed training group, who learn the pairs for one 15-minute session (just writing them out on scrap paper over and over again), and a spaced training group, who learn the same pairs for three sessions of 5 minutes each. You could give them 30 pairs to learn and test them (say after a 10-minute break after the last session) on all 30 pairs. This would be an independent measures design and your hypothesis would predict a one-tailed difference between the two groups on their recall scores.

7. Variations of the Stroop effect

The Stroop effect is said to be an example of an automatic process – for example, how difficult it is to avoid reading text that is put in front of you. The effect occurs when lists of colour words are presented, with each word being printed in either the same colour as the word (the word "red" in red ink – the word–colour congruent condition) or in a different colour (the word "red" printed in blue ink, the incongruent word–colour condition). The task is to name the *colour of the ink*. This is easy in the congruent condition but more difficult in the incongruent condition, where the colour of the ink and the colour word are different. The ease or difficulty of the task is measured as the time taken to name the colour of the ink. Normally participants are shown a list of words in the congruent condition, and are tested on how long it takes to read all of the words, and are then given a list of words in the incongruent condition, and are tested on how long it takes them to read this list. Notice that counterbalancing is crucial here otherwise very sizeable order effects emerge.

    You could do a modification of the Stroop effect by using less-common colours and colour names, as well as common colour names. The theory of automatic processing would predict that the less-common colours are not processed in such an automatic fashion as very common colours. So, for example, you could use colours such as mauve, peach, mint, but allow participants to name the colour using their own words (so the word "mauve" written in a mint colour could still be named as green). The prediction is that the time difference between congruent and incongruent trials on common colours will be greater than the time difference between congruent and incongruent trials on uncommon colours. So, for each participant you record their mean time taken for each congruent trial and subtract this from their mean time taken for each incongruent trial for the common colours. You do the same for uncommon colours and you then have two sets of data for each participant. Your hypothesis is therefore one-tailed and predicts a difference in this repeated measures experiment.

8. The effects of context on perception

Several famous studies have shown that context can affect how something is perceived. For example, when shown in a series of numbers, 13 can be interpreted as thirteen, but when shown in a series of letters it can be interpreted as B. Other studies have shown that an ambiguous drawing can be interpreted in a way that depends on what has been shown previously. For example, a drawing that can be interpreted either as an old man or as a rat, is perceived differently depending on whether pictures of people or pictures of animals have previously been shown.

You can devise your own investigation on such context effects in perception by using what are known as "homophones". These are words that can be spelt in two different ways to mean two different things. For example, *ail* and *ale* are both pronounced in exactly the same way but are spelt diffently and mean different things. You could select a list of homophones around a theme, such as war and violence, and give your participants text to read that is either a description of a battle scene or a description of something unrelated to war and violence, such as gardening. Homophones you could use are arms–alms, beat–beet, bury–berry, bite–byte (or bight), break–brake, die–dye, fought–fort, knight–night, naval–navel, pain–pane, war–wore, and so on. Mix these words up with other unrelated (non-homophonic) words. These words are read out to participants who then have to write them down. It is likely that they will write down the first meaning of the homophone that comes to mind. The context of the battle story should, if context theory is correct, prime them to write down the war/violence meaning of the homophone, more so than participants who have read the gardening story. If you want to check out more or different homophones try: http://www.bifroest.demon.co.uk/misc/homophones.html. This would be a one-tailed hypothesis of differences and the design would be independent measures.

9. Extraversion, introversion, and problem solving

According to Eysenck's theory of personality, extraverts are said to:

- talk a lot and be spontaneous;
- dislike working alone;
- be very expressive with their body movement, such as their hands;
- prefer a lot of activity;
- like getting praise and enjoy competitions;
- like to go for the quick solution;
- have excellent short-term memory;
- like things to be colourful, loud, and exciting.

If such a personality dimension exists, then introverts who are more careful in their thinking, take more time to work out a solution, and are less distracted by excitement should solve problems that require these characteristics more quickly than extraverts. One such problem is the candle problem, which is said to demonstrate *functional fixedness*. Introverts should be less likely than extraverts to fall prey to functional fixedness, or should they? One could always argue that since extraverts crave excitement they may look at the problem in a more novel way than introverts, and hence find the solution to the candle problem more quickly.

The idea for the investigation would be to present the candle problem to a number of participants. In this problem, participants are asked to imagine that they have been asked to attach a candle to a wall over a table so that the wax did not drip onto the table below. The only objects in the room are: the candle, a box of tacks, matches, a small number of other objects that are of no use for solving the task, and a table. Solutions most commonly given are either to glue the candle to the wall by melting some of it or to tack the candle directly to the wall. Few think of using the tack box as a candle holder, and this is because participants' perception of the tack box is "fixated" on its use as a container for tacks and cannot be reconceptualised to solve the problem. In your study you could measure the time taken to produce the best solution (with a time-out if they cannot find a solution, say 10 minutes). Then administer a form of the extravert/introvert scale of the EPI. One version can be found at: http://www.trans4mind.com/questionnaire/

The analysis would involve a correlation of time taken with extraversion score. The two-tailed hypothesis predicts a correlation but not whether it is positive or negative.

10. The National Lottery and the representativeness heuristic

In terms of how people make decisions, the representativeness heuristic is the tendency to choose an option that is more consistent with experience. In other words, typical instances of a category are thought to be more likely to occur than examples that are not typical. For example, when asked which is the more likely birth order of six children, boy-girl-boy-girl-boy-girl or boy-girl-girl-girl-girl-girl, most people respond with the first sequence. However, the chances of the two sequences are the same. People make their choice because the first seems more representative of the population, which is more or less half male and half female.

A modern version of the representativeness heuristic would be to present sets of possible lottery numbers, divided into numbers randomly but fairly evenly spaced (spaced numbers) and numbers that are lumped together (skewed numbers). An example of spaced numbers would be 3, 14, 19, 28, 35, 42, and an example of skewed numbers would be 12, 13, 14, 15, 17, 19. Both sets of numbers are equally likely to occur in the National Lottery draw. However, will people be more willing to choose spaced numbers than skewed numbers because these are more representative of the winning numbers that have come up before? The task involves people choosing between two sets of numbers on each trial. One set consists of spaced numbers, the other skewed numbers. You could devise up to 20 or so trials and count the percentage of spaced numbers chosen by each participant.

If you think about it, there may be some individual differences in this task. For example, would a student of maths make the same choices as a student of art? You could choose both types of student as your participants. For this investigation the hypothesis is a one-tailed prediction of differences between two independent groups (maths versus art students). The rationale might be to test the notion that people generally tend to use the representativeness heuristic unless they have precise, expert knowledge of the subject (but it would still be interesting if maths students chose more spaced numbers too!).

11. Is the outcome of the Wason selection task dependent on the concreteness of the material?

The Wason selection task was designed to test deductive reasoning. Deductive reasoning is about how the rules of logic can be used to draw conclusions about the truth or falsehood of a conclusion given a number of premises. Here's an example of a premise: *If it is raining outside then you need to put up your umbrella*. Notice that it is of the form if (something) then (something else). Suppose we know that *it is raining*; then can we conclude that *you need to put up your umbrella* is true or false? It is true, because the conclusion is consistent with the premise.

Now, in logic there is something called *modus ponens*. It is simply the rule that it is not logical to work back from an if-then type of relationship. So, if we knew that *you need to put up your umbrella*, would it be logical to conclude that *it is raining outside*? You may be tempted to think "yes". However, it is false because there could be many other reasons why you have to put your umbrella up – it might be snowing, there might be a burst water main, it might be very sunny and hot, or you might just want to put up your umbrella for no obvious reason. So, when we have a premise if (something) then (something else) we cannot conclude that if (something else) is true then so must (something) be true, and this is called modus ponens.

The Wason selection task is actually set up to get people to make the modus ponens error. Participants are shown four cards each with either a letter or number printed on the face: R, G, 2, and 7. The participant is told that "If there is an R on one side of the card then there is a 2 on the other side of the card". The task is to select only those cards that need to be turned over in order to test the truth or falsehood of the statement. Most people choose R and 2. However, the correct answer is R and 7. R needs to be turned over and that is quite obvious; 2 is irrelevant because if there is an R on the other side the rule is confirmed but if there is a G the rule is not disconfirmed, since we cannot work back as in modus ponens (it is as if 2 = *you need to put up your umbrella* and R = *if it is raining outside*), so G is irrelevant (since G could be equal to *it's snowing outside*). However, the case of 7 is different, because if there is an R on the other side of it, then this will disconfirm the statement.

Wason and colleagues have claimed that the reason why people make the mistake is because they look to *confirm* statements rather than to *disconfirm* statements. However, the problem is also rather abstract (which you will know if you found the above difficult to follow) and Wason and Shapiro found that the task is much easier if the four cards say Manchester, Leeds, car, and train, and the task is to discover the truth of the statement "Every time I go to Manchester I travel by car". A more concrete version of the task is easier.

It is possible to derive even more concrete versions of the task, such as four cards with Dave, Steve, Trudie, Vicky, and the statement "Dave has only been married to Vicky". Which two cards should be turned over now? Dave has to be turned over, but not Steve because Dave can't marry Steve (at least not in the UK). Trudie needs to be turned over because she may have been married to Dave. Vicky doesn't need to be turned over because Vicky could have married someone else as well as Dave (well, not at the same time, at least in the UK). The question is, given that this is a more concrete example of the Wason selection task, do more people solve it correctly than the Manchester-by-car example or the original example?

Your hypothesis would be a one-tailed prediction of differences and the data you collect will be categorical (the number who got Manchester-by-car correct and the number who got it wrong, and the number who got Dave-Vicky correct and the number who got it wrong).

12. Is personality a concrete measure or does it depend on the situation?

Trait theories of personality – that is, those based on questionnaire measurements, such as Eysenck – assume that personality is fairly stable and changes little from situation to situation. In this view, personality is an inner essence of a person and can be objectively measured regardless of the situation. In contrast, Mischel (1993) has argued that personality is more fluid, since people behave differently and take on different attitudes depending on the situation. This "situationalist" view holds that people's behaviour is not consistent across different situations and largely depends on the context.

If people behave differently in different situations then it follows that they behave differently depending on whom they are with. This theory then predicts that the perception of a colleague or good friend (but not a very close friend) about a person's personality should be measurably different from that of the person's mother, father, or close relative. You could test this theory for your investigation by doing the following:

1. Identify a dozen or so participants.
2. Each participant should identify a very close relative and a good friend (but not their best friend or a very close friend).

3. Identify and locate a suitable personality questionnaire.
4. Get the close relative and the friend to complete the questionnaire *on behalf of the participant*. In other words, they complete it by answering questions about the participant.

The prediction is that the measures of the person's personality should be different between the close relative's assessment and the friend's assessment. You could test for a correlation between the two questionnaire results, with the one-tailed prediction of trait theory that the two measures should correlate positively. If no significant correlation is found, then the results would be more consistent with situationalism than with trait theory. Different subscales on the EPI can be found at http://www.trans4mind.com/questionnaire/

13. Personality questionnaires, self-assessment, and a short-cut?

One thing that has always struck me about questionnaires is whether they really need to be so lengthy. For example, Eysenck's EPI has 57 questions in all. Under half of these relate to extraversion/introversion. Now, since a questionnaire is a self-report measure, the question is whether it could be replaced by one's own self-report to *one* question. For example, the concept extraversion–introversion can be defined as:

> Extraversion is characterised by being outgoing, talkative, high on positive affect (feeling good), and in need of external stimulation. According to Eysenck's arousal theory of extraversion, there is an optimal level of cortical arousal, and performance deteriorates as one becomes more or less aroused than this optimal level. Arousal can be measured by skin conductance, brain waves or sweating. At very low and very high levels of arousal, performance is low, but at a more optimal mid-level of arousal, performance is maximised. Extraverts, according to Eysenck's theory, are chronically under-aroused and bored and are therefore in need of external stimulation to bring them up to an optimal level of performance. Introverts, on the other hand, are chronically over-aroused and jittery and are therefore in need of peace and quiet to bring them up to an optimal level of performance.
>
> (Shepherd, 2004)

You could provide this (or a better) description to your participants and get them to rate themselves on a 10-point scale, such as 1 = I'm a total extravert, to 10 = I'm a total introvert, and 5 = I'm half extravert and half introvert. You can encourage them to use any point between 1 and 10 that best describes how extraverted/introverted they are. Next, they complete the extraversion/introversion subscale of the EPI. Once you've gathered the data you do a test of correlation. If trait theories of personality have any validity then there should be a strong positive correlation between the two measures, and if there is a strong correlation then one could ask whether the one-question method could be used to replace the lengthy version.

14. Gender stereotyping

There are numerous studies that could be carried out on this subject, from observations to discourse analysis, and using children or adults as participants. For example, you could videotape two 12–18-month-old children playing alone – of course, ethical issues arise, and you must have permission to do this. One is a boy and one is a girl and both are wearing neutral colours (non-gender-stereotyped colours or patterns). The viewer has to say which is the boy and which is the girl. You could analyse how often men were correct against how often women were correct and do a chi-square test on the data. You could also ask them some questions afterwards to find out on what basis they made their decisions. This should be interesting because boys and girls generally tend to be quite indistinguishable at that age.

Another idea is to present young children a range of toys and ask them which toys boys like to play with and which girls like to play with. You could compare different age groups to see if older children make finer discriminations than younger children.

Looking at older children, you could ask them for their favourite television programmes and classify their responses as (a) the main character is female, (b) the main character is male, (c) the main character is neither male nor female or there is only one character. To obtain more data, you could ask them for their two favourite programmes. You could even ask them for their least favourite programme. The prediction is that most boys will prefer programmes where the main character is male and girls will prefer programmes where the main character is female. There are many studies on the influence of television on gender identity and your study could add some interesting findings to the issue.

15. Are boys anti-intellectualists?

Girls are beginning to outshine boys in nearly all A level subjects (Eysenck, 2004). The question is what are the reasons for this trend? A recent article on the BBC news website (http://news.bbc.co.uk/1/hi/education/3494490.stm) covers this question and cites research by Draves and Coates that it is the curriculum that is responsible for the gap between girls and boys, rather than anything else. Many boys, they argue, are viewing the curriculum as irrelevant; while they are spending many hours of their spare time on computers they are preparing themselves well for "knowledge jobs". The curriculum, on the other hand, aims to prepare them for "industrial jobs".

In order to assess these questions, you could design a survey that asks about boys' perception of different subjects, homework, teachers, and whether school provides them with the skills they think are necessary for a successful working life. You could also include some questions that tap into anti-intellectual feelings, such as whether being a scientist, researcher, news reporter, and so on are worthy careers. You could also ask about whether they feel youth culture (music, magazines, favourite websites, and so on) has any influence on their attitudes to school.

16. Group socialisation and peer influence

According to Harris (1998), adolescent children are shaped more by their peers than they are by their parents or siblings. Although siblings share genetic similarities and environmental similarities (e.g., the home), they are often very different from each other. Harris claims that this theory explains these differences.

One way of testing this is to devise an experiment whereby adolescent children have to rate a series of drawings or photographs. They are told how different groups of people feel towards the pictures by seeing a rating level for each group. So, for example, a picture of clown is shown and ratings (out of 10) for the picture made by different groups are shown next to the picture. The participant then has to rate the picture himself or herself. The group ratings that are shown could be taken from different age groups or from predefined groups such as primary school girls, primary school boys, senior school girls, grandparents, teachers, and so on. Don't have too many groups, though, otherwise the analysis will be very intensive! The idea is to correlate the participants' ratings with that of each group. Do the participants' ratings correlate more strongly with children of their own age group and sex (namely, their peers) than with any other group? The prediction is that the correlation between the participants' ratings and those of their peer group will be more positive than the correlation between the participants' ratings and those of a different group.

An alternative to doing a correlation would be to calculate difference scores between the participants' ratings and the ratings of one group (e.g., teachers) and the difference between the participants' ratings and a second group (e.g., same-age children). You could then carry out a test of difference between the scores from the two comparisons: Suppose participant 1 rated picture 1 as 6. Suppose he is told that Group 1 (teachers) gave it a 4 rating. The participant–teacher difference score is 2. Suppose the participant is told that Group 2 (peers) gave it 7, then the participant–peer score is 1 (ignore whether the Group rating is higher or lower than the participants' rating, just note the actual difference). Then for each participant, add up all of the teacher difference scores and all of the peer difference scores and compare them. The hypothesis would be a one-tailed prediction of differences between the two sets of scores and the design is repeated measures.

17. The Social Readjustment Scale and stress levels

Holmes and Rahe (1967) developed the Social Readjustment Rating Scale to identify the sorts of events that can cause people stress. You could devise an experiment to compare students who have different stress levels on their score on this scale. You could use the listing on page 466 of Eysenck (2004) or look at:
http://chipts.ucla.edu/assessment/Assessment_Instruments/
Assessment_files_new/assess_srrs.htm

Ask your participants a simple question to divide them into different stress groups, such as "How stressed have you felt this week?" with three options: *very much*, *moderately*, and *only a little*. Use the answer to this question to divide your participants into the three groups. Then get them to complete the Social Readjustment Rating Scale by listing the 40+ items (but mix them up). The participant ticks each one that they have experienced in the last 12 months. Compare the stress scores of the two most extreme groups – the very-much responders (the stress group) and the only-a-little responders (the no-stress group). Ignore the middle group because it is often more fruitful to compare the extreme groups. The hypothesis would be a one-tailed prediction that the stress group will score higher overall on the scale than the no-stress group. Such a finding would add validity to the scale. Failure to find differences would cast doubt on the validity of the scale, especially for the sample you have tested.

18. Testing the phonological loop

According to Alan Baddeley, the phonological loop was theorised, in part, to account for the finding that information in short-term memory is coded phonemically. For example, when *seeing* a list of words, mistakes in recall are often based on the *sounds* of the words, that is, mistakes are based on the phonemic structure of the word. It is theorised that when reading words, people subvocally articulate the words (say them in their heads). However, when participants are prevented from rehearsal the effect of acoustic/phonemic similarity disappears, but only for visually presented words. Errors of recall for acoustically similar items with auditory presentation are not eliminated when participants are prevented from rehearsal.

A relatively straightforward replication that tests the phonological loop hypothesis is the following. Devise two lists of words or letters that are either acoustically similar (E, B, P, T, C, D, G, V) or dissimilar (Q, W, R, Y, U, O, S, F) and present each list with alternating similar–dissimilar items (e.g., E, Q, B, R, T, Y) and also the other way round (U, C, O, D, S, G). Present several trials of each by reading out the list to your participants and asking them to recall the list in the exact order in which you read it (create your answer sheet in a way that forces them to try to reproduce the order, e.g., by using a blank box for each item and each trial, and where they have to write out one letter per box). You will need two groups of participants. For one group, at the end of each trial they simply write down the items. It is likely that this group will start rehearsing the items the moment you stop calling out the last item (rehearsal group). For another group, during each trial the participant must repeat the word "the" over and over until you have finished reading out the list. The purpose of this task (called articulatory suppression) is to eliminate rehearsal, so this group is the no-rehearsal group.

Score each answer sheet according to whether the item is acoustically similar or acoustically different. In other words, for each participant, find the mean number of errors made on acoustically similar and acoustically different items. Then find the means of both groups. There will be two hypotheses, both one-tailed, that are consistent with the theory of working memory. The first hypothesis predicts that there should be no differences in the number of errors made on acoustically similar and acoustically different items for the no-rehearsal group (this will be one test of difference). The second hypothesis predicts that there should be significant differences in the number of errors made on acoustically similar and acoustically different items for the rehearsal group (this will be a second test of difference).

Failure to support the hypotheses would provide difficulties for the theory. If you want to try a variation of the experiment, you could think of other ways of preventing rehearsal, such as counting backwards in threes, or you could try using words, or even long words, in the lists.

19. A test of levels of processing theory

Levels of processing theory was developed as an alternative to the idea that the primary resource in recall is rehearsal. It was argued that the deeper the level of processing, the better something will be remembered. A deep level of processing is when something is learned in terms of its meaning – the more meaning attached to the items, the better they will be remembered. For example, words that rhyme (shallow level) are supposed to be harder to recall than words that are related by what they mean (deep level).

As a test of the levels of processing account of memory, you could present two groups of participants with the same list of words but with a different learning method. For the shallow group the words are merely written down and studied. For the deep group the participant is required to create a "mind map" – words written inside different shapes, with lines connecting words by meaning. Both groups are presented with several lists and are given the same time to write out and study the words. The hypothesis would be a one-tailed prediction that the deep group will recall significantly more words than the shallow group.

20. Emotional factors in memory: State-dependent memory and flashbulb memory

Emotion is supposed to be a major cause of being able to recall something (as in studies of flashbulb memory) and a major cause of forgetting something (such as in the Freudian concept of repression). You could divide participants into high and low emotion groups by reading out a description of what it means to be an emotional person and getting them to rate themselves on a scale of 1 to 10, with 1 = *I am not an emotional person*, 5 = *I am quite an emotional person*, and 10 = *I am a very emotional person*.

A definition of an emotional person might be:

> A person who has a strong tendency to regard things emotionally, that is someone who responds and perceives the world around them in terms of whether they imply happiness, sadness, joy, anxiety, and so on. This kind of person would find it hard to just "stick to the facts". An emotional person displays their emotion openly and sometimes to the point that they seem to overindulge in displays of emotion.

The group that self-rate themselves the highest are the high emotional group, and the lowest are the low emotional group. There are several ways in which you could use both groups.

First, you could give them a test of recall for lists of emotion words (e.g., laugh, cry, sad, and so on) and non-emotion words (e.g., bind, jade, from, and so on). Mix up the types of words and test for recall. Give several lists so that you gather a good amount of data per participant. The one-tailed hypothesis will be that the high emotional group will recall more emotion words that the low emotional group. You could link this study with theories of mood-state-dependent memory.

A second way to use the groups would be to present them with an emotionally provocative video (but be careful about the ethics of showing violent scenes, or explicit love scenes; check out the material with your tutor before proceeding). Devise 20 questions about things that went on in the video clip, 10 of these should concern non-emotional aspects of the clip and 10 emotional aspects of the clip. The hypothesis could be one-tailed, and predict that the high emotional group will get more of the 10 emotion questions correct than will the low emotional group. You could link this study with the literature on eyewitness testimony.

References

Andrade, J. (2001). *Working memory in perspective*. Hove, UK: Psychology Press.

Asch, S.E. (1946). Forming impressions of personality. *Journal of Abnormal and Social Psychology, 41*, 258–290.

Baddeley, A., Thomson, N., & Buchanan, M. (1975). Word length and the structure of short-term memory. *Journal of Verbal Learning and Verbal Behavior, 14*, 575–589.

Baddeley, A.D., & Hitch, G.J. (1974). Working memory. In G.A. Bower (Ed.), *Recent advances in learning and motivation* (Vol. 8, pp. 47–90). New York: Academic Press.

Beck, A.T., Epstein, N., Brown, G., & Steer, R.A. (1988). An inventory for measuring clinical anxiety: Psychometric properties. *Journal of Consulting and Clinical Psychology, 56*, 893–897.

Crick, F., & Mitchison, G. (1983). The function of dream sleep. *Nature, 30.* 111–114.

Davis, S. (1990). Men as success objects and women as sex objects. *Sex Roles, 23*(1–2), 43–50.

DeLongis, A., Coyne, J.D., Dakof, G., Folkman, S., & Lazarus, R.S. (1982). Relationship of daily hassles, uplifts and major life events to health status. *Health Psychology, 1*(2), 119–136.

Eysenck, M.W. (2004). *Psychology for A2 level*. Hove, UK: Psychology Press.

Eysenck, H.J., & Eysenck, S.B.G. (1975). *The Eysenck Personality Questionnaire*. London: Hodder & Stoughton.

Fisher, R.A. (1956). *Statistical methods and scientific inference*. New York: Hafner.

Franken, R.E. (1988). *Human motivation* (2nd Ed.). Pacific Grove, CA: Brooks/Cole.

Harris, J.R. (1998). *The nurture assumption: Why children turn out the way they do*. New York: Free Press.

Holmes, T.H., & Rahe, R.H. (1967). Social readjustment rating scale. *Journal of Psychosomatic Research, 11*, 23–28.

Howell, D.C. (1997). *Statistical methods for psychology* (4th Ed.). Belmont, CA: Duxbury Press.

Keppel, G. (1967). A reconsideration of the extinction-recovery theory. *Journal of Verbal Learning & Verbal Behavior, 6*(4), 476–486

Latané, B., & Darley, J.M. (1970). *The unresponsive bystander: Why doesn't he help?* Englewood Cliffs, NJ: Prentice Hall.

Lewinsohn, P.M. (1974). A behavioral approach to depression. In R.M. Friedman & M.M. Katz (Eds.), *The psychology of depression: Contemporary theory and research*. New York: Wiley.

Lieberman, D.J. (2000). *Learning: Behavior and cognition* (3rd Ed.). Belmont, CA: Wadsworth.

Loftus, E.F. (1975). Leading questions and the eyewitness report. *Cognitive Psychology, 7*, 560–572.

Lorge, I. (1930). Influence of regularly interpolated time intervals upon subsequent learning. *Contributions to Education* (Whole No. 438). New York: Columbia University, Teachers College.

Luchins, A. (1957). Primacy–recency in impression formation. In C.I. Hovland (Ed.), *The order of presentation in persuasion*. New Haven, CT: Yale University Press.

Milgram, S. (1965). Some conditions of obedience and disobedience to authority. *Human Relations, 18*, 57–76.

Mischel, W. (1993). *Introduction to personality* (5th Ed.). Fort Worth, TX: Harcourt Brace.

Neath, I. (1998). *Human memory: An introduction to research, data, and theory*. Belmont, CA: Brooks/Cole Publishing Co.

Shepherd, P. (2004). *The Eysenck Personality Questionnaire*. Available online: http://www.trans 4mind.com/personality/EPQ.html. Accessed December 2004.

Spielberger, C.D. (1983). *Manual for the State-Trait Anxiety Inventory (STAI)*. PaloAlto, CA: Consulting Psychologists Press.

Thurlow, C., & Brown, A. (2003). Generation Txt? The sociolinguistics of young people's text-messaging. Available online: http://www.shu.ac.uk/daol/articles/v1/n1/a3/thurlow 2002003-paper.html. Accessed 5 May 2005.

Tolman, E.C. (1938). The determinants of behavior at a choice point. *Psychological Review, 45*, 1–41.

Underwood, B.J. (1961). Ten years of massed practice on distributed practice. *Psychological Review, 68*, 229–247.

Webb, W.B., & Cartwright, R.D. (1978). Sleep and dreams. In M. Rosenzweig & L. Porter (Eds.), *Annual Review of Psychology, 29*, 223–252.

Weiner, M.J., & Wright, F.E. (1973). Effects of underlying arbitrary discrimination upon subsequent attitudes toward a minority group. *Journal of Experimental Social Psychology, 3*, 94–102.

Wright, D. (2003). Making friends with your data: Improving how statistics are conducted and reported. *British Journal of Educational Psychology, 73*, 123–136.

Zimbardo, P.G. (1973). On the ethics of intervention in human psychological research: With special reference to the Stanford Prison Experiment. *Cognition, 2*, 243–256.

Zuckerman, M. (1979). *Sensation seeking: Beyond the optimal level of arousal*. Hillsdale, NJ: Lawrence Erlbaum Associates Inc.

Appendix 1
Coursework specifications

What is this appendix about?

The specifications – coursework requirements and the marking criteria – for a number of GCSE, AS, and A2 courses are summarised in this appendix. Read the text relating to your course to find out what you have to do and how your work will be marked. This appendix provides you with the coursework details for the following courses/specifications:

- AQA GCSE Psychology
- AQA GCE AS/A2 Psychology (Specification A)
- AQA GCE AS/A2 Psychology (Specification B)
- OCR GCSE Psychology
- OCR GCE AS/A2 Psychology
- EDEXCEL GCE AS/A2 Psychology
- SQA Higher Psychology

While these details were correct, as far as the author is aware, at the time of going to press, there may be one or two last-minute alterations that you need to be aware of. Always consult your tutor about specification details in case of any recent changes.

Course: AQA GCSE (2005)

What are the aims of the coursework?
One of the key aims of the course is for students to gather information, analyse it in a critical manner, and use evidence to back up arguments. Gathering information refers in part to the act of carrying out an investigation in psychology, i.e., testing participants in an experiment or other research method. Critical analysis is about not taking information at face value or accepting an argument or claim without looking at potential pitfalls or weaknesses. It is also about being

self-critical. This means that your own research is also open to criticism and you can provide this criticism yourself, since it will show that you have good analytical skills.

How much will your coursework count towards your final grade?
The coursework represents 20% of the overall GCSE Psychology mark.

What do you have to do?
You will need to produce a practical report of one research investigation, designed and carried out by yourself. You should choose a suitable subject matter in psychology, and it should be located within the subject specification. Note that it must be necessarily psychological – comparing men and women on how much they spend on clothes might be an interesting subject, but is it necessarily psychological?

What should the length of the report be?
The report should be no more than 1000 words in length.

Can you work in groups?
Data used for the study must be recorded by you, and not by your participants or your class.

Who marks your work?
Your teacher assesses your work. It will also be externally moderated by AQA, which means that a teacher or lecturer from another school or college will be appointed by AQA to look at your work to agree the marks.

Which method should you use?
You can use an experiment, survey, observation, case study, or a correlational design. You must seek the guidance and supervision of your tutor before undertaking your study.

Which statistics are you expected to use?
You will be expected to use at least two of the following: mean, mode, median, range, and percentages. Presenting your summary data in a table and a graph will also be expected.

Which topics can you investigate?
You should choose a subject located within the subject specification.

How will your work be marked?

Your report should consist of the following headings: Introduction, Method (with subsections Design, Participants, Materials, Procedure), Results, Discussion. Marks are allocated according to each section.

- Introduction (3 marks)
- Method (13 marks)
  - Design (5 marks)
  - Participants (2 marks)
  - Materials (2 marks)
  - Procedure (4 marks)
- Results (9 marks)
- Discussion (10 marks)
- Quality of written communication (5 marks)

The relevant chapters of this book will tell you how to organise your report this way and what to put in each section.

Which parts of the coursework carry the most and least marks?

Take a look at the distribution of marks and you will soon realise that 65% of the final marks are awarded for the rationale, design, and evaluation of the study. The Results section accounts for about 22% of the final mark. Therefore, the bulk of the marks concern the quality of the rationale you have provided for your investigation, the actual design you have developed, and how you interpreted and evaluated the findings of your study.

Course: AQA GCE AS/A2 (2005) Specification A

Note: AQA provide two different specifications, A and B. Specification A draws on a broader range of issues and perspectives in psychology (five main areas, as opposed to three in Specification B). Specification B differs from Specification A in that it has a stronger scientific/ practical emphasis than Specification A.

What are the aims of the coursework?

One of the key aims of the course is to prepare students for higher education. In terms of coursework this means that you will learn how to carry out research using well-established methods in psychology and you will gain some experience of reporting your research in a way that is appropriate for the scientific study of psychology.

How much will your coursework count towards your final grade?

The coursework counts as 15% of the total A-level grade, and is taken within the A2 component of the course.

What do you have to do?

You will need to produce a project brief and a practical report of a research investigation, carried out by you. You should choose a suitable subject matter in psychology, and it should be located within the subject specification. The project brief is to be written before you begin work on the practical (see below).

What should the length of the coursework be?

The project brief is written by filling in the form provided for you. The maximum length of the report is 2000 words.

Can you work in groups?

For your investigation you are allowed to seek detailed advice from your teacher or tutor. You will be allowed to work in a group of up to four, with the design and so on being the work of the group. Each student should write his or her own report. However, the extent to which you have sought advice from your teacher and the extent to which you have worked as a group will be reflected in the marks you will be given. The more independently you have worked, the more marks you can get. This is clearly a matter of personal choice. If you are not confident that you can design and carry out the study by yourself, you have to weigh up the dangers of getting anxious and confused by working alone against the loss of a possible three marks here (and three marks for the next element *The appropriateness of the design*) for seeking a lot of advice or for working in a group.

Who marks your work?

The work is assessed by your teacher and externally moderated by AQA, which means that a teacher or lecturer from another school or college, and appointed by AQA, will look at the work to agree the mark.

What methods can you use?

Your investigation must use one of the following research methods: a laboratory, field, or natural experiment, a survey, an observational study, or a correlational method.

Which statistics are you expected to use?

You will be expected to use appropriate descriptive statistics (such as the mean, median, mode, range, or percentages), and you will be expected to present summary data in tables and graphs. You will also be expected to use inferential statistics, where appropriate. Examples of inferential tests given by AQA are: chi-square, the binomial sign test, the Wilcoxon matched-pairs test, the Mann-Whitney U test or Spearman's rho. Other more advanced tests could also be used, such t-tests, but students would not be expected to use advanced tests such as ANOVA or factor analysis.

What topics can you investigate?

Your investigation must be necessarily psychological and has to be located in one of the areas listed in the AQA (A) Specification, either AS or A2.

How will your work be marked?

You have to complete both a project brief *and* a final report. The project brief has to be written *before* you carry out your investigation. The reason for this is so that you are more clear about what it is you are trying to achieve and what you intend to do before you begin collecting data (it also encourages good practice).

The project brief

The project brief is done by completing a form, which your teacher or tutor should provide for you. You will be asked to provide the following details about your study (the maximum marks for each part are shown in brackets):

- A statement of the hypothesis (No marks are allocated, but the hypothesis still needs to be stated!)
- An explanation of the direction of the hypothesis (1 mark)
- A statement about your research method and design (1 mark)
- A statement about the advantages and disadvantages of the method (2 marks)
- A statement about what the bias or confounding variables might be (2 marks)
- A statement of how you plan to control for bias or confounding variables (2 marks)
- A statement of your statistical significance level (1 mark)
- A statement of ethical considerations (3 marks)

The report

The final report should have the following headings: Abstract, Introduction, Aims and Hypotheses, Method (although not explicitly stated in the AQA specification guidelines, it is standard practice to include the subsections: Design, Participants, Materials, Procedure), Results, Discussion, References.

- Your contribution to the design (3 marks)
  - The extent to which you have sought advice from your teacher and the extent to which you have worked as a group will be reflected in the marks you will be given. The more independently you have worked, the more marks you can get.
- The appropriateness of the design (3 marks)
- Your abstract (3 marks)
- Introduction (5 marks)
- Formulation of the aims and hypothesis/hypotheses (3 marks)
- Reporting the method (4 marks)
- Selection and application of statistics (4 marks)
  - You will be expected to apply two types of statistics: descriptive and inferential
- Presentation of the data (4 marks)
- Discussion: Your explanation of the findings (3 marks)
- Discussion: Relationship of the findings of your study with previous research (3 marks)
- Discussion: Limitations and modifications (3 marks)
- Discussion: Implications and suggestions for further research (3 marks)
- References (2 marks)
- Report style (3 marks)

The relevant chapters of this book will tell you how to organise your report this way and what to put in each section.

Which parts of the coursework carry the most and least marks?

The most heavily weighted element within the coursework report appears to be related to the Method (which includes issues surrounding the design of the study), and accounts for over 25% (or more than a quarter) of the total coursework marks. The next most important element is the Discussion section of the written report.

It is also worth pointing out that if your contribution is minimal (i.e., you have worked as a group and with help from the tutor) you could lose about 10% of the total possible marks, so you can take this into account when trying to assess how much help you wish to accept.

Course: AQA GCE AS/A2 (2005)
Specification B

Note: Specification B differs from Specification A in that it has a stronger scientific/practical emphasis than Specification A. In addition, Specification B draws on three main areas of psychology, compared to five in Specification A.

What are the aims of the coursework?
One of the key aims of the course is to provide a solid foundation for students wishing to enter higher education. In terms of coursework this means that you will learn how to carry out research and will develop skills such as the analysis, interpretation, and evaluation of information.

How much will your coursework count towards your final grade?
There are two requirements for coursework in Specification B of the AS/A2 level. The first is a component of the AS specification and represents 30% of the total AS mark (15% of the total A-level mark). The second is a component of the A2 specification and represents 15% of the total A-level mark. The AS practical is assessed by an external tutor appointed by AQA, while the A2 practical is assessed by your teacher or tutor.

AS practical investigation (AS Module 3)
AQA Specification B

What do you have to do?
You will be required to carry out and report on an investigation in psychology.

What should the length of the coursework be?
The final report of the investigation that you submit should be between 1500 and 2000 words in length, not including appendices.

Can you work in groups?
You are not allowed to work in groups, and your investigation must be entirely your own work.

Who marks your work?
The AS practical is assessed by an external tutor appointed by AQA.

Which methods can you use?
Your investigation must use any suitable psychological method of inquiry.

Which statistics are you expected to use?
You will be expected to use appropriate descriptive statistics, and these should be presented according to report-writing conventions in psychology. All calculations should be shown in a separate appendix at the end of the report.

Which topics can you investigate?
Your investigation must be necessarily psychological and has to be located in one of the areas listed in the AQA (B) specification for AS (modules 1 and 2).

How will your work be marked?
AQA breaks up the assessment aims for the AS coursework through four skills, A, B, C, and D. Your markers will be looking for all four when allocating marks to your coursework.

Skill A: Design (28 marks). Marks are allocated for:

- The aim of the investigation in the Introduction
- Your review of background material to the study, i.e., previous research on the issue
- The hypothesis/hypotheses of your study
- Your statement of the variables under investigation (e.g., what the dependent and independent variables are)
- Extraneous variables you have identified
- For each extraneous variable identified, what suitable experimental controls you have in place
- Choice of sample
- The nature of the task given to participants, as well as the materials used
- Any ethical issues relevant to your study that you have identified
- The clarity of the description of the procedure

Skill B: Implementation (4 marks). Marks are allocated for:

- Evidence in your report that your treatment of participants was appropriate
- Evidence in your report that you carried out appropriate procedures

Skill C: Analysis and interpretation (20 marks). Marks are allocated for:

- The clarity and appropriateness of the data you present in your report
- The appropriateness and formatting of any tables, graphs, or charts you use to present summary data
- The appropriateness and correctness of any statistical test used
- The clarity of your summary of the data
- The relevance and accuracy of the way you relate the results to the hypothesis
- The extent to which you relate the results to the background research
- The relevance of the conclusions you draw from your study
- Whether you identified the limitations of your study
- Your suggestions for improvements to your study if repeated
- Your suggestions for further research

Skill D: Communication (8 marks). Covers the following points:

- That every section is included
- Your communication of ideas and use of appropriate psychological terms
- The clarity of the abstract
- Appropriateness of your References section

Which parts of the coursework carry the most and least marks?
If you include the marks for implementation, then the design aspects of your investigation count for more than 50% of the marks for your practical investigation (32 out of 60). Your analysis, or Results section, will account for 33% of the total marks. It is clear, then, that you must put a lot of work into choosing the right topic, since you will need to create a well-designed investigation in order to get good marks. You should therefore consider aspects of the design very carefully and logically.

A2 coursework (A2 Module 6) AQA Specification B

What do you have to do?
You must carry out and report on one investigation. The report must contain the following sections: Abstract, Introduction, Method (Design, Participants, Materials, Procedure), Results, Discussion, and References.

What should the length of the report be?
Your report should be between 2000 and 2500 words in length, not including appendices.

Can you work in groups?
You are allowed to work in small groups in the design and implementation of the study, but the report you submit must be entirely your own work – that is, your report should only be similar to those of others in your group in that it is based on the same design and data. The final report of the investigation is written solely by you and in your own words. The extent to which you worked as part of a group is taken into account in marking. You can lose marks depending on how much you relied on the work of the other members of the group (see below).

Who marks your work?
The A2 practical is assessed by your teacher or tutor.

Which methods can you use?
You can choose any suitable psychological method of inquiry.

Which statistics are you expected to use?
You will be expected to calculate and present both descriptive and inferential statistics. The inferential test you use should be appropriate for the data you have obtained.

Which topics can you investigate?
Your investigation must be necessarily psychological and has to be located in one of the areas listed in the AQA (B) specification for A2 (modules 4 and 5). It must also be done on a *different topic* from that chosen for module 3 from the AS specification, that is, the topic for your AS coursework.

How will your work be marked?

Marking is divided into four sections: Design, Implementation, Analysis and interpretation, and Communication. Marking criteria are provided for each section, and your report will be marked by your tutor or teacher and then externally moderated by AQA moderators. The marking criteria are as follows:

Design

- Relevance of background material (4 marks)
- Formulation of aims (2 marks)
- Statement of hypotheses (2 marks)
- Design decisions (4 marks)
- Ethical considerations (4 marks)
  - You should adhere to these guidelines and there should be statements in your design section on how you did this, any potential problems that may have arisen, and how you dealt with them. If appropriate, you should include all of the instructions given to your participants. If these are lengthy you could include them in the appendices.
- Independence in the design of the study (3 marks)
  - If you designed the study entirely on your own then you will be awarded 3 marks.
  - If you designed your study in a small group, and the design is sufficiently original (i.e., not an exact replication of a previous study) then you will be awarded 2 marks.
  - If you have (either in a small group or on your own) decided to replicate a previous study then you will be awarded 1 mark.
  - If you have made no contribution at all to the design then you will be awarded 0 marks.
  - If you are not confident about designing your own study then you should consider working in a small group. One has to weigh up the loss of only a few marks with a good design against gaining a few marks but having a weak or flawed design. On the whole, the latter could lose you more marks than the former.

Implementation

- Implementation of design decisions (3 marks)
  - Design elements are clear and well thought out.
- Dealing with participants (3 marks)
- Independence in conducting the study (2 marks)
  - As with the design of the study you will lose or gain marks

depending on whether you worked on your own or in a group.

- ○ If you carried out the study yourself (that is, created the materials on your own and tested all of the participants yourself) then you will be awarded 2 marks.
- ○ If you carried out the study in a small group (and actively got involved) then you will be awarded 1 mark.
- ○ If you worked in a small group but didn't get involved in carrying out the study then you will not get any marks.
- ○ As with the design criterion above, you should weigh up the pros and cons of working by yourself or in a small group. If the method is particularly time consuming or the number of participants required is large then it may be worthwhile to work in a small group. Of course, in order to do so, the group would need to have the same design, which means that you could lose up to 3 marks if you include the loss of marks for designing the study in a group. This is a small price to pay, in my view, if testing participants is going to be too time consuming for you.

Analysis and interpretation

- Data analysis (4 marks)
- Presentation of data (4 marks)
- Explanation of the results (3 marks)
- Relationship to background material (3 marks)
- Implications of the results (2 marks)
- Limitations (2 marks)
- Suggestions for improvements (2 marks)
- Suggestions for further research (2 marks)

Communication

- Written aspects (3 marks)
- Quality of communication (3 marks)
- Abstract (3 marks)
- References (3 marks)

Which parts of the coursework carry the most and least marks?

Most marks are allocated to the design aspects of the report and the writing-up of the Methods section. The next most important section is the Discussion. Clearly, you need to create a well-designed investigation in order to get good marks. You should consider aspects of the design very carefully and logically. You will also be expected to appraise your method and findings competently.

Course: OCR GCSE Psychology (Component 5)

What are the aims of the coursework?
The main aim of the course itself is to give students the opportunity to study psychology at an introductory level. The coursework will allow you to go into more detail on a particular topic that is listed in the subject specification.

How much will your coursework count towards your final grade?
The coursework counts for 20% of the final GCSE grade.

What do you have to do?
You must carry out and report on one investigation in psychology.

What should the length of the report be?
It should be no longer than 1500 words in length, not including references, appendices, graphs, and tables.

Can you work in groups?
You are allowed to work in small groups in order to design and carry out the investigation, but your report should be written up by you in your own words and not by the group.

Who marks your work?
The report is marked by your teacher or tutor.

Which methods can you use?
You may choose any suitable psychological method of inquiry. Methods suggested by OCR are experimental method, observational method, correlational study, survey, and content analysis study.

Which statistics are you expected to use?
You will be expected to use descriptive statistics (means, medians, modes) to summarise the data, and the use of tables, pie-charts, graphs and so on will get extra marks.

Which topics can you investigate?
Your investigation must be necessarily psychological and has to be located in one of the areas listed in the specification.

How will your work be marked?
OCR divides its marking criteria into five categories, mostly reflecting the sections of the final report:

1. Introduction: The ability to link the aims of the investigation with psychological theory (9 marks)
2. Method: The ability to use appropriate and replicable psychological research methods (9 marks)
3. Results: The ability to collect, analyse, and present data (8 marks)
4. Discussion: The ability to analyse and interpret research findings (9 marks)
5. Presentation: The ability to communicate ideas effectively (5 marks)

Which parts of the course carry the most and least marks?
If the marks for presentation are shared evenly between each of the main sections then your Introduction, Method, Results, and Discussion sections are just about equally weighted. This means that half of the total possible marks are allocated to the mechanics of your investigation (design and data-analysis aspects) and the other half to the more literary aspects (literature review and rationale, and your evaluation of the study).

Course: OCR GCE AS/A2 Psychology

What are the aims of the coursework?
The aims of the coursework are to allow students to experience the process of data collection and analysis, as well as how to interpret data and identify the strengths and weaknesses of a variety of psychological research methods.

How much will your coursework count towards your final grade?
There are two levels of coursework for the OCR AS/A2 courses. The AS coursework accounts for 16.7% of your final A-level grade, as does the A2 coursework (hence about one third of your A-level grade is based on your coursework).

AS course

What do you have to do?
For the AS course the practical work involves four data-collection exercises. You will have to write the Method and Results for each, and

these form your practical work folder, which you later take into your examination as a memory aid. It should be noted that your practical folder (which is provided to your school or college by OCR) should not contain more information than that indicated in the guidelines; otherwise it could give you an unfair advantage over other students in the exam. Practical folders are left in the examination room and samples are examined by OCR, so don't be tempted to add extra notes.

The four data-collection exercises consist of the following:

- *Activity A: Questions, self-reports, and questionnaires.* You will learn about the types of questions used in each type and the sorts of rating scales used. Notes on these can be recorded in the practical folder.
- *Activity B: Observation.* You will learn about how human behaviour can be categorised and the rating or coding systems used, and also of alternative ways of sampling the same behaviour. Only notes on coding systems can be recorded. The remainder must not be recorded, according to the OCR specification.
- *Activity C: Data collection of differences between two groups.* You will learn how to compare data from two groups of participants, using an inferential test, such as the Mann-Whitney U test or a Wilcoxon signed ranks test. The calculations of this, or a computer printout of the calculations, should be recorded in the practical folder.
- *Activity D: Collection of data suitable for a test of correlation.* You will learn how to carry out a test of correlation on two sets of data. The calculations of this, or a computer printout of the calculations, should be recorded in the practical folder.

How will your work be marked?
You take the practical folder into the exam with you to help you recall details of the practical activities you did in class. You can use the folder to help you answer the questions in the exam. It is important that you adhere to the guidelines provided by your tutor, since OCR do not provide further details of these activities. As this work is not marked directly, we will not discuss it in any further detail in this section. Instead, you can refer to methodological chapters of this book to help you understand the different methods in psychological research.

The assignment

For your written assignment you are required to apply psychological concepts and theories to an everyday event.

What should the length of the assignment be?

Your written assignment must be no longer than 1000 words, not including references.

Can you work in groups?

You are not allowed to work in groups, but you are allowed to discuss the nature of your assignment with your tutor.

Who marks your work?

An external tutor, appointed by OCR, will mark your work.

Which topics can you investigate?

The topic or event must be carefully chosen, you must not break ethical principles, and the work must not be offensive in any way (e.g., racially or sexually offensive). In discussion with your teacher or tutor, you should identify a psychologically relevant event (an event that could be understood using existing psychological theories and concepts). A copy of the source (e.g., newspaper article) has to be included with your report. The source must not be longer than two pages of a tabloid newspaper, or three A4 pages of a website.

How will your work be marked?

Your assignment begins with a statement about the source of the event (e.g., "Why I Refused to Eat for 5 Days", *Cosmopolitan*, June issue, 2000). You will then need to address three questions:

1. What are the underlying psychological assumptions in or the issues raised by the source?
2. Describe and relate some psychological evidence to the source.
3. How can psychological evidence be used to address the issues raised in the source?

The marking criteria are as follows:

- Issues, assumptions (9 marks)
  - The event you choose should raise a number of issues from at least two areas in psychology.

- You should justify and make clear what the relationship is between the event and relevant psychological issues and concepts.
- Evidence (15 marks)
  - You should provide evidence from the psychological literature of any issues or explanations you raise.
  - Such discussion should be directly related to the event and not tangential.
  - In doing this you should also demonstrate your understanding of a range of psychological concepts, theories, and perspectives.
- Applications (10 marks)
  - You should demonstrate good knowledge of psychology (breadth and depth), especially that which directly relates to the event.
  - You should demonstrate the ability to bring appropriate psychological evidence to the issue as well as an understanding of how to apply and evaluate psychological issues and concepts.
- Presentation and communication (6 marks)
  - The assignment should be coherent and concise, meaning that it should be well focused on a handful of appropriate psychological issues and your work should have a logical flow to it.
  - You should show a good understanding of psychological terms and you should not use them out of place (for example, don't follow weak or tenuous links).
  - The text should contain a good number of references and these should be listed in the references section (which itself must be written in the correct format).

Course: EDEXCEL GCE AS/A2

What are the aims of the coursework?
The aims of the coursework are to give students experience with the process of gathering data and the opportunity to write a research report.

How much will your coursework count towards your final grade?
The coursework is Unit 3 of the AS level, and contributes to one third of the AS mark, or if you take A2 the following year it will contribute to just over 16% of the final A-level grade.

What do you have to do?
You must carry out and report on one investigation using any psychological method of inquiry, suitable for gathering quantitative data.

This means that you can carry out an experiment or observation, say, but not a method for obtaining qualitative data, such as discourse analysis.

What should the length of the report be?
The report should be between 1500 and 2000 words in length, not including references, appendices, graphs, and tables.

Can you work in groups?
You are allowed to work in small groups in order to design and carry out the investigation, but your report should be written up by you and not by the group.

Who marks your work?
The report is marked by an EDEXCEL appointed tutor.

Which methods can you use?
Methods suggested by EDEXCEL are a field or natural experiment, a correlation, a naturalistic observation, a questionnaire or survey, or a content analysis.

Which statistics are you expected to use?
You are required to calculate and present descriptive statistics. The use of tables, charts, and graphs to present summary data is encouraged. You do not need to concern yourself with inferential statistics.

Which topics can you investigate?
Your study should adhere to the ethical guidelines of the British Psychological Society. Failure to follow these guidelines could result in your work being failed, regardless of the quality of the rest of your work. Although not stated explicitly in the specification, I suggest you choose a topic that is covered in the course.

How will your work be marked?
Your work must be set out with the following headings (marks are given against each section):

- Introduction
  - Background research (10 marks)
  - Rationale (4 marks)
  - Aims of the study (2 marks)
  - Hypothesis (2 marks)

- Method
  - Method and design (2 marks)
  - Variables (2 marks)
  - Participants (2 marks)
  - Apparatus (2 marks)
  - Procedure (4 marks)
  - Controls (2 marks)
- Results
  - Summary table (2 marks)
  - Summary table commentary (2 marks)
  - Additional graph or chart, plus accompanying commentary (2 marks)
  - Descriptive statistics commentary (2 marks)
  - Relationship of the results to the hypothesis (3 marks)
- Discussion
  - Validity (4 marks)
  - Suggestions for improved validity (4 marks)
  - Reliability (4 marks)
  - Suggestions for improved reliability (4 marks)
  - Implications of the study (4 marks)
  - Generalisation of findings (2 marks)
  - Application of study to everyday life (2 marks)
- References and appendices (3 marks)
- Presentation of the report (2 marks)

Which parts of the coursework carry the most and least marks?
There is a very high percentage of marks given to the Discussion section. This means that for your EDEXCEL marker, your ability to appraise and evaluate your own research is highly valued. This is likely to be because one of the most important aspects of being a psychologist is being able to interpret research findings and understand a piece of research in its broader context, i.e., how research is used to develop explanations of human behaviour. It is therefore very clear that you should devote a good portion of your coursework efforts to learning how to produce the right kind of discussion. Even more interesting is the fact that since the coursework counts as just over 16% of your final A-level grade, the Discussion section alone counts for about 6% of your final grade. One implication of this is that a discussion that satisfies all of the marking criteria could quite easily raise your A-level grade from, say, a C to a B, or a B to an A.

Also note that the Results section counts for only 17% of your coursework mark (about 3% of your final A-level grade). This means that if you are not very confident with data analysis and your Results section is fair at best, it won't have a dramatic effect on your final grade. So for those students who find statistics difficult and anxiety-inducing, fear not. Do your best but don't lose any sleep over it. Try to compensate for this by producing a good discussion.

Course: SQA Higher Psychology

What are the aims of the coursework?
The main aims are to assess your skills in applying psychological research methods, and your ability to integrate the knowledge gathered in the course, especially your ability to evaluate research and analyse data.

How much will your coursework count towards your final grade?
The coursework counts for 20% of the grade.

What do you have to do?
You will need to produce a report of a research investigation carried out by you. You should choose a suitable subject matter in psychology, and it should be located within the subject specification.

What should the length of the report be?
The length of the report should be between 1500 and 2000 words.

Can you work in groups?
You are allowed to work in groups from the design of the study to the collection of data. However, your report must be your own and not written together. The teacher or tutor is allowed to give you some guidance on the writing of your report (e.g., he or she can comment on your draft).

Who marks your work?
The work is assessed externally by SQA, which means a teacher or lecturer from another school or college, and appointed by SQA, will mark your work.

What methods can you use?
Your investigation must use one of the following research methods: a laboratory, field, or natural experiment, a survey, an observational study, interview, or a correlational method.

Which statistics are you expected to use?

You will be expected to use appropriate descriptive statistics (such as the mean, median, mode, range, percentages, range, and standard deviation), and you will be expected to present summary data in tables and graphs. You will *not* be expected to use inferential statistics, although you can use them if you wish. According to the specification, you will lose a lot of marks if you use inferential statistics inappropriately, so only use them if you are confident with them.

What topics can you investigate?

Your investigation must be necessarily psychological and has to be located in one of the optional units listed in the SQA specification. The topic may be chosen by your tutor.

How will your work be marked?

Your report should have the following headings:

- Title (1 mark)
- Abstract (2 marks)
- Introduction (6 marks)
- Method (4 marks). Use the subheadings: Design, Participants, Apparatus/Materials, and Procedure.
- Results (5 marks)
- Discussion (6 marks)
- Conclusion (2 marks)
- References (2 marks)
- Appendices (2 marks)

Which parts of the coursework carry the most and least marks?

If we group the Introduction and the Discussion, then nearly 50% of the marks are devoted to providing analysis and evaluation of theories, other research, and your own study. Just under a quarter of the marks are allocated to the title, Abstract, References, and Appendices. The Method and Results sections, where you demonstrate skills in research design and statistics, account for just over a quarter of the total marks. The emphasis, then, is clearly on the more "textual" sections, so you need to show a good understanding of the purpose of research and its relation to theory development.

Appendix 2

Statistical tables

Appendix 2a: Sign test

To use the table, first identify the correct row, which is the value you have for N. Next look down the column that represents the value you have for S. The cell where the column and row meet contains the probability of obtaining that value of S for that value of N. For example, if $S = 8$, and $N = 27$, then the cell value is 0.026, thus the probability of $S = 8$, with $N = 27$ is 0.026. This means that you can write the result as "According to the sign test, the difference between the scores from the two conditions is statistically significant at the 5% level. For $N = 27$ the probability of $S = 8$ is 0.026 ($p < 0.05$, one-tailed)."

If you had a two-tailed hypothesis then in the above example you would multiply the cell value by 2 (i.e., $0.026 \times 2 = 0.052$) and you could write "According to the sign test, the difference between the scores from the two conditions is just outside statistical significance at the 5% level. For $N = 27$ the probability of $S = 8$ is 0.052 ($p > 0.05$, two-tailed)."

For values not shown here you can use the calculator freely available at: http://www.graphpad.com/quickcalcs/welcome.htm

When the page opens, select "GraphPad QuickCalc", choose "categorical data", and then choose "Binomial & sign test".

Alternatively, it is possible to calculate p values not shown here using Excel. To do this:

1. Open an Excel worksheet and click on an empty cell.
2. Click the equals sign in the Formula Bar.
3. Click the down arrow to search for the function which you will find in "More Functions . . ."
4. Choose BINOMDIST.
5. In the cell labelled "Number_S" enter your S value.
6. In the cell labelled "Trials", enter your N value.

Computed probabilities (one-tailed) for the sign test. For two-tailed probabilities, multiply the cell value by 2.

Values of S

N	1	2	3	4	5	6	7	8	9	10	11	12	13	14	15	16	17	18	19
6	0.109	0.344	0.656																
7	0.062	0.227	0.5																
8	0.035	0.144	0.363	0.637															
9	0.019	0.09	0.254	0.5															
10	0.011	0.055	0.172	0.377	0.623														
11	0.006	0.033	0.113	0.274	0.5														
12	0.003	0.019	0.073	0.194	0.387	0.613													
13	0.002	0.011	0.046	0.133	0.291	0.5													
14	0.001	0.006	0.029	0.09	0.212	0.395	0.605												
15	<0.001	0.004	0.018	0.06	0.151	0.304	0.5												
16	<0.001	0.002	0.011	0.038	0.105	0.227	0.402	0.598											
17	<0.001	0.001	0.006	0.024	0.072	0.166	0.314	0.5											
18	<0.001	0.001	0.004	0.015	0.048	0.119	0.24	0.407	0.593										
19	<0.001	<0.001	0.002	0.01	0.032	0.084	0.18	0.324	0.5										
20	<0.001	<0.001	0.001	0.006	0.021	0.058	0.132	0.252	0.412	0.588									
21	<0.001	<0.001	<0.001	0.004	0.013	0.039	0.095	0.192	0.332	0.5									
22	<0.001	<0.001	<0.001	0.002	0.009	0.026	0.067	0.143	0.262	0.416	0.584								
23	<0.001	<0.001	<0.001	0.001	0.005	0.017	0.047	0.105	0.202	0.339	0.5								
24	<0.001	<0.001	<0.001	<0.001	0.003	0.011	0.032	0.076	0.154	0.271	0.419	0.581							
25	<0.001	<0.001	<0.001	<0.001	0.002	0.007	0.022	0.054	0.115	0.212	0.345	0.5							
26	<0.001	<0.001	<0.001	<0.001	0.001	0.005	0.014	0.038	0.084	0.164	0.279	0.422	0.578						

27	<0.001	<0.001	<0.001	0.003	0.01	0.026	0.061	0.124	0.221	0.351	0.5						
28	<0.001	<0.001	<0.001	0.002	0.006	0.018	0.044	0.092	0.172	0.286	0.425	0.575					
29	<0.001	<0.001	<0.001	0.001	0.004	0.012	0.031	0.068	0.132	0.229	0.356	0.5					
30	<0.001	<0.001	<0.001	<0.001	0.003	0.008	0.021	0.049	0.1	0.181	0.292	0.428	0.572				
31	<0.001	<0.001	<0.001	<0.001	0.002	0.005	0.015	0.035	0.075	0.14	0.237	0.36	0.5				
32	<0.001	<0.001	<0.001	<0.001	0.001	0.004	0.01	0.025	0.055	0.108	0.188	0.298	0.43	0.57			
33	<0.001	<0.001	<0.001	<0.001	<0.001	0.002	0.007	0.018	0.04	0.081	0.148	0.243	0.364	0.5			
34	<0.001	<0.001	<0.001	<0.001	<0.001	0.002	0.004	0.012	0.029	0.061	0.115	0.196	0.304	0.432	0.568		
35	<0.001	<0.001	<0.001	<0.001	<0.001	<0.001	0.003	0.008	0.021	0.045	0.088	0.155	0.25	0.368	0.5		
36	<0.001	<0.001	<0.001	<0.001	<0.001	<0.001	0.002	0.006	0.014	0.033	0.066	0.122	0.202	0.31	0.434	0.566	
37	<0.001	<0.001	<0.001	<0.001	<0.001	<0.001	0.001	0.004	0.01	0.024	0.049	0.094	0.162	0.256	0.371	0.5	
38	<0.001	<0.001	<0.001	<0.001	<0.001	<0.001	<0.001	0.002	0.007	0.017	0.036	0.072	0.128	0.209	0.314	0.436	0.564
39	<0.001	<0.001	<0.001	<0.001	<0.001	<0.001	<0.001	0.002	0.005	0.012	0.027	0.054	0.1	0.168	0.261	0.375	0.5
40	<0.001	<0.001	<0.001	<0.001	<0.001	<0.001	<0.001	0.001	0.003	0.008	0.019	0.04	0.077	0.134	0.215	0.318	0.438

This table was compiled by the author.

7. In "Probability_S" enter 0.5 (this is always 0.5 for the sign test)
8. In "Cumulative" enter FALSE.
9. Click OK.
10. The result is a numerical value between 0 and 1 that is the corresponding p value. The value shown is for a one-tailed hypothesis, and for a two-tailed hypothesis this value should be multiplied by 2.
11. If the final p value is less than 0.05 then the result is statistically significant.

Appendix 2b: The Wilcoxon matched-pairs signed ranks test

To use the table, identify the row corresponding to the N value you have. Beginning with the right-most column, identify whether the value of T you have obtained is *less* than the cell value. If it is greater than the cell of the right-most column then examine the next column and so on until you have found the column whose cell value is greater than your obtained value. If you cannot find a value then the result is not statistically significant at least at the 5% level. For a one-tailed hypothesis refer to the columns identified by the row labelled "One-tailed" and for a two-tailed hypothesis refer to the columns identified by the row labelled "Two-tailed".

For example, for N = 9 and T = 6, we look up the first column and identify the row with the value 9. The cells in the other columns are: 8, 5, 3, and 1. Since our T value is only less than the first cell value (i.e., 8) and since that column refers to a one-tailed hypothesis at 0.05, then our result is statistically significant at the 0.05 level. We can therefore write: "According to the Wilcoxon matched-pairs signed ranks test, the difference between the scores from the two conditions is statistically significant at the 5% level. For N = 9 the critical value for the smaller T is 8 at the 5% level ($p < 0.05$, one-tailed). As the observed value of T (6) is less than the critical value there is a less than 5% probability that the observed difference is due to chance. Since the difference is statistically significant and since the mean of condition 1 is higher than the mean of condition 2, the null hypothesis is rejected and the experimental hypothesis is accepted."

For values of N not listed here, or if you would prefer to calculate actual p values then you can do the calculations for free at: http://department.obg.cuhk.edu.hk/researchsupport/Wilcoxon.asp

When the page loads, enter your data in columns and click "Do Wilcoxon". It is not possible to calculate actual probabilities in Excel for this test (at least not in the version that I have, which is 9.0.3821).

Critical values of T for a one- and two-tailed hypothesis.

T value				
One-tailed	$p < 0.05$	$p < 0.025$	$p < 0.01$	$p < 0.005$
Two-tailed		$p < 0.05$	$p < 0.025$	$p < 0.01$
N				
5	0			
6	2	1		
7	3	2	0	
8	5	3	1	0
9	8	5	3	1
10	10	8	5	3
11	13	10	7	5
12	17	13	9	7
13	21	17	12	9
14	25	21	15	12
15	30	25	19	15
16	35	29	23	19
17	41	34	27	23
18	47	40	32	27
19	53	46	37	32
20	60	52	43	37
21	67	58	49	43
22	75	65	55	48
23	83	73	62	54
24	91	81	69	61
25	100	89	76	68
26	110	98	84	75
27	119	107	92	83
28	130	116	101	91
29	140	126	110	100
30	151	137	120	109
31	163	147	130	118
32	175	159	140	128
33	187	170	151	138
34	200	182	162	148
35	213	195	173	159
36	227	208	185	171
37	241	221	198	182
38	256	235	211	194
39	271	249	224	207
40	286	264	238	220

This table was compiled by the author.

Appendix 2c: The Mann-Whitney U test

Critical values at 0.05 for Na and Nb for a one-tailed hypothesis.

Na \ Nb	1	2	3	4	5	6	7	8	9	10	11	12	13	14	15	16	17	18	19	20
1	–	–	–	–	–	–	–	–	–	–	–	–	–	–	–	–	–	–	–	–
2	–	–	–	–	–	–	–	0	0	0	0	1	1	1	1	1	2	2	2	2
3	–	–	–	–	0	1	1	2	2	3	3	4	4	5	5	6	6	7	7	8
4	–	–	–	–	–	–	3	4	4	5	6	7	8	9	10	11	11	12	13	13
5	–	0	1	2	2	3	5	6	7	8	9	10	12	13	14	15	17	18	19	20
6	–	–	–	–	–	5	6	8	10	11	13	14	16	17	19	21	22	24	25	27
7	–	–	–	–	–	–	8	10	12	14	16	18	20	22	24	26	28	30	32	34
8	–	–	–	–	–	–	–	13	15	17	19	22	24	26	29	31	34	36	38	41
9	–	–	–	–	–	–	–	–	17	20	23	26	28	31	34	37	39	42	45	48
10	–	–	–	–	–	–	–	–	23	26	29	33	36	39	42	45	48	52	55	
11	–	–	–	–	–	–	–	–	–	30	33	37	40	44	47	51	55	58	62	
12	–	–	–	–	–	–	–	–	–	–	37	41	45	49	53	57	61	65	69	
13	–	–	–	–	–	–	–	–	–	–	–	45	50	54	59	63	67	72	76	
14	–	–	–	–	–	–	–	–	–	–	–	–	55	59	64	67	74	78	83	
15	–	–	–	–	–	–	–	–	–	–	–	–	–	64	70	75	80	85	90	
16	–	–	–	–	–	–	–	–	–	–	–	–	–	–	75	81	86	92	98	
17	–	–	–	–	–	–	–	–	–	–	–	–	–	–	–	87	93	99	105	
18	–	–	–	–	–	–	–	–	–	–	–	–	–	–	–	–	99	106	112	
19	–	–	–	–	–	–	–	–	–	–	–	–	–	–	–	–	–	113	119	
20	–	–	–	–	–	–	–	–	–	–	–	–	–	–	–	–	–	–	127	

This table was compiled by the author.

To use the table, identify the row and column corresponding to the Na and Nb value you have. Identify whether the value of U you have obtained is *less* than the cell value. If it is then it is significant at the 0.05 level, otherwise it is not statistically significant.

If you wish to calculate actual probabilities for both one- and two-tailed hypotheses, you can do so by visiting: http://eatworms. swmed.edu/~leon/stats/utest.html

Appendix 2d: The *t*-test

To use this table, identify the degrees of freedom (df) and find the corresponding row. Find the cell that is furthest to the right whose value is less than the value of *t* obtained in your study. The level of significance is then indicated by the column label, depending on whether your hypothesis is one- or two-tailed.

If you wish to calculate actual probabilities you can do so in Excel.

1. Enter the data for one group or condition in column A, one score per cell.
2. Enter the data for the other group or condition down column B.
3. Click on an empty cell.
4. Click the equals sign on the Formula Bar.
5. Select the down arrow to show functions available to you and select "More Functions . . .".
6. Under functions choose TTEST.
7. For "Array 1" select all of the cells of column A (e.g., you could enter A1:A13 if you had 13 participants).
8. For "Array 2" enter the cells of column B (e.g., B1:B13).
9. For "Tails" enter whether your hypothesis is one-tailed or two-tailed.
10. Under "Type" enter 1 if the *t*-test is related (paired or repeated measures) or enter 2 if it is unrelated (or independent measures).
11. Click OK.
12. The value in the cell is the computed *p* value. If the *p* value is less than 0.05 the difference between the means of the two groups is statistically significant.

Critical values for a one- and two-tailed *t*-test.

Two-tailed	$p = 0.10$	$p = 0.05$	$p = 0.02$	$p = 0.01$
One-tailed N−1 (df)	$p = 0.05$	$p = 0.025$	$p = 0.01$	$p = 0.005$
1	6.314	12.706	31.821	63.657
2	2.92	4.303	6.965	9.925
3	2.353	3.182	4.541	5.841
4	2.132	2.776	3.747	4.604
5	2.015	2.571	3.365	4.032
6	1.943	2.447	3.143	3.707
7	1.895	2.365	2.998	3.499
8	1.86	2.306	2.896	3.355
9	1.833	2.262	2.821	3.25
10	1.812	2.228	2.764	3.169
11	1.796	2.201	2.718	3.106
12	1.782	2.179	2.681	3.055
13	1.771	2.16	2.65	3.012
14	1.761	2.145	2.624	2.977
15	1.753	2.131	2.602	2.947
16	1.746	2.12	2.583	2.921
17	1.74	2.11	2.567	2.898
18	1.734	2.101	2.552	2.878
19	1.729	2.093	2.539	2.861
20	1.725	2.086	2.528	2.845
21	1.721	2.08	2.518	2.831
22	1.717	2.074	2.508	2.819
23	1.714	2.069	2.5	2.807
24	1.711	2.064	2.492	2.797
25	1.708	2.06	2.485	2.787
26	1.706	2.056	2.479	2.779
27	1.703	2.052	2.473	2.771
28	1.701	2.048	2.467	2.763
29	1.699	2.045	2.462	2.756
30	1.697	2.042	2.457	2.75
40	1.684	2.021	2.423	2.704
60	1.671	2	2.39	2.66
120	1.658	1.98	2.358	2.617

This table was compiled by the author.

Appendix 2e: Spearman's rho

Critical values for Spearman's rho test.

One-tailed test	0.05	0.025	0.01	0.005
Two-tailed test	0.1	0.05	0.02	0.01
N				
8	0.643	0.738	0.833	0.881
9	0.600	0.683	0.783	0.833
10	0.564	0.648	0.745	0.858
11	0.520	0.620	0.737	0.814
12	0.496	0.591	0.703	0.776
13	0.475	0.566	0.673	0.743
14	0.456	0.544	0.646	0.714
15	0.440	0.524	0.623	0.688
16	0.425	0.506	0.602	0.665
17	0.411	0.490	0.583	0.644
18	0.399	0.475	0.565	0.625
19	0.388	0.462	0.549	0.607
20	0.377	0.450	0.535	0.591
21	0.368	0.438	0.521	0.576
22	0.359	0.428	0.508	0.562
23	0.351	0.418	0.497	0.549
24	0.343	0.409	0.486	0.537
25	0.336	0.400	0.476	0.526
26	0.329	0.392	0.466	0.515
27	0.323	0.384	0.457	0.505
28	0.317	0.377	0.448	0.496
29	0.311	0.370	0.440	0.487
30	0.305	0.364	0.433	0.478
35	0.282	0.336	0.400	0.442
40	0.263	0.314	0.373	0.412
45	0.248	0.295	0.351	0.388
50	0.235	0.280	0.333	0.368
60	0.214	0.255	0.303	0.335
70	0.198	0.236	0.280	0.310
80	0.185	0.221	0.262	0.290
90	0.174	0.208	0.247	0.273
100	0.165	0.197	0.234	0.259

This table was compiled by the author.

To use the table, identify the row corresponding to the N value you have. The value of Spearman's rho obtained in your study should be greater than (or equal to) the value in the cell.

While you are encouraged to calculate the test by hand, you can check your calculations by conducting the test in Excel. To do this:

1. In Excel enter the scores on variable 1 in column A.
2. Enter the scores on variable 2 in column B.
3. Click on an empty cell.
4. Click the equals sign on the Formula Bar.
5. Select the down arrow to show functions available to you and select "More Functions . . .".
6. Under functions choose CORREL.
7. For "Array 1" select all of the cells of column A (e.g., you could enter A1:A13 if you had 13 participants).
8. For "Array 2" enter the cells of column B (e.g., B1:B13).
9. Click OK.

The value shown is the correlation coefficient rho (and not the computed significance level – to check the significance level look up the value in the above table).

Appendix 2f: Chi-square test

Critical values for the chi-square test.

df	0.05	0.025	0.01	0.005
1	3.84	5.02	6.24	7.88
2	5.99	7.38	9.21	10.60
3	7.82	9.35	11.34	12.84
4	9.49	11.14	13.28	14.86
5	11.07	12.83	15.09	16.75
6	12.59	14.45	16.81	18.55
7	14.07	16.01	18.48	20.28
8	15.51	17.53	20.09	21.95
9	16.92	19.02	21.67	23.59
10	18.31	20.48	23.21	25.19
11	19.68	21.92	24.72	26.76
12	21.03	23.34	26.22	28.30
13	22.36	24.74	27.69	29.82
14	23.68	26.12	29.14	31.32
15	25.00	27.49	30.58	32.80
16	26.30	28.85	32.00	34.27
17	27.59	30.19	33.41	35.72
18	28.87	31.53	34.81	37.16
19	30.14	32.85	36.19	38.58
20	31.41	34.17	37.57	40.00
21	32.67	35.48	38.93	41.40
22	33.92	36.78	40.29	42.80
23	35.17	38.08	41.64	44.18
24	36.42	39.36	42.98	45.56
25	37.65	40.65	44.31	46.93
26	38.89	41.92	45.64	48.29
27	40.11	43.19	46.96	49.64
28	41.34	44.46	48.28	50.99
29	42.56	45.72	49.59	52.34
30	43.77	46.98	50.89	53.67

This table was compiled by the author.

To use the table, identify the row corresponding to the degree of freedom (df) of your study (in most cases this will be 1). Determine whether the value you have obtained is greater than the values shown in that row. Begin by comparing your obtained value with the value in the right-most cell and continue to the left cell, until you find a value that is less than your obtained value.

You are encouraged to calculated by hand, however, it is possible to check your results online. Go to: http://www.graphpad.com/quickcalcs/contingency1.cfm

Enter your observed values as a contingency table and choose "Chi-square with Yates' correction". Click "Calculate" and the test returns the value of chi and its corresponding significance value.

Index